CROSS-COUNTRY SKI TOURS

CROSS-COUNTRY SKI TOURS

WASHINGTON'S
South Cascades & Olympics
SECOND EDITION

Tom Kirkendall & Vicky Spring

THE
MOUNTAINEERS

Published by
The Mountaineers
1001 SW Klickitat Way, Suite 201
Seattle, Washington 98134

9 8 7 6 5
5 4 3 2 1

Published simultaneously in Canada by Douglas & McIntyre, Ltd., 1615 Venables Street, Vancouver, B.C. V5L 2H1

Published simultaneously in Great Britain by Cordee, 3a DeMontfort Street, Leicester, England, LE1 7HD

Printed in Canada

Edited by Dana Lee Fos
Maps by Tom Kirkendall
All photographs by the authors
Cover design by The Mountaineers Books
Book design and typesetting by The Mountaineers Books
Book layout by Gray Mouse Graphics
Cover photograph: *Skier near the summit of Amabilis Mountain (Tour 15)*
Frontispiece: *Skier on route from Corral Pass to Mutton Mountain; Mount Rainier in distance (Tour 36)*

Library of Congress Cataloging-in-Publication Data

Kirkendall, Tom.
    Cross-country ski tours—Washington's south Cascades and Olympics / Tom Kirkendall & Vicky Spring.
        p.   cm.
    Rev. ed. of: Cross-country ski tours of Washington's south Cascades and Olympics. c1988.
    Includes bibliographical references (p.   ) and index.
    ISBN 0-89886-415-1
    1. Cross-country skiing—Washington (State)—Olympic Mountains—Guidebooks.   2. Cross-country skiing—Cascade Range—Guidebooks.   3. Olympic Mountains (Wash.)—Guidebooks.   4. Cascade Range—Guidebooks.   I. Spring, Vicky, 1953–   .   II. Kirkendall, Tom.   Cross-country ski tours of Washington's south Cascades and Olympics.   III. Title.
    GV854.5.W33K567   1995
    917.97'5—dc20
                                                          95–23137
                                                             CIP

CONTENTS

HIGHWAY 410—WEST

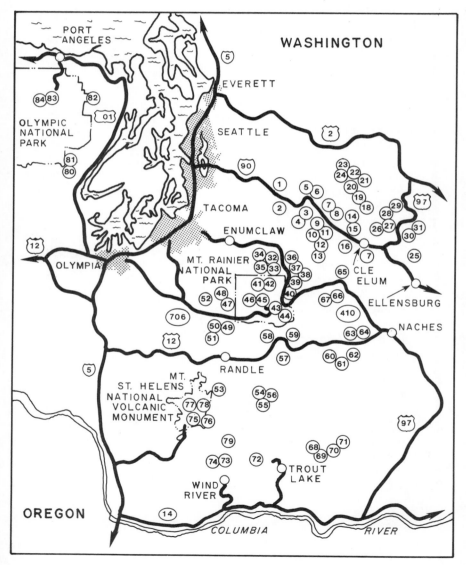

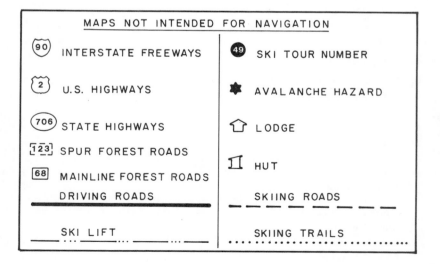

MAPS NOT INTENDED FOR NAVIGATION

(90) INTERSTATE FREEWAYS

(2) U.S. HIGHWAYS

(706) STATE HIGHWAYS

[123] SPUR FOREST ROADS

[68] MAINLINE FOREST ROADS

DRIVING ROADS

SKI LIFT

49 SKI TOUR NUMBER

✹ AVALANCHE HAZARD

⌂ LODGE

Ⅱ HUT

SKIING ROADS

SKIING TRAILS

THE CROSS-COUNTRY SKIERS' SCORE BOARD

In the earlier editions of this book we used the preface to make note of the giant disparity between the amount of area set aside for motorized winter recreation and the amount of area reserved for nonmotorized winter use. We also stressed that there are no guarantees that we will be able to preserve the space we do have for the quiet winter traveler. In this edition we intend to not only reiterate the problems but also point out the successes.

Once again, we need to stress that our winter wonderland does not come with a guarantee. Just because there was a Sno-Park at the start of a tour last year does not guarantee parking there this year. And even though you took the entire Scout troop for an affordable tour this year, you may have to pay a fee to ski in the same place next year. National Parks are not immune to the pressures of the well-financed snowmobile lobby, and you may find that where you once worried only about tangling skis and snowshoe tracks you now must leap out of the way of speeding machines.

These examples refer to real problems faced by skiers in the last few years. The Crystal Springs/Stampede Pass Sno-Park, which provided parking for 42,000 visitors in 1993, was closed in 1994 when its 5-year lease was not renewed. The Mill Creek Sno-Park on the east side of Stevens Pass has been given over to a private corporation, and you must fork over a daily trail fee to ski up that beautiful valley. The Hyak–Rocky Run Sno-Park at Snoqualmie Pass may eventually be phased out as private developers take over the area. And the once great skiers' sanctuary of Mount Rainier National Park now allows snowmobiles up Stevens Canyon Road as far as Box Canyon.

On the positive side of the ledger, skiers can applaud and enjoy the gargantuan efforts of the Mt. Tahoma Trails Association, who in the face of incredible odds have created an exciting trail and hut system on public and private land near Mount Rainier. You may add your support to their efforts by skiing on the scenic trails and by volunteering to help with the constant upkeep involved. The Mount Adams and Wind River Ranger Districts of the Gifford Pinchot National Forest also deserve a round or two of heartfelt applause, and three very lively cheers for their energetic efforts in creating new skiers' Sno-Parks and marking trails that are reserved for skiing and nonmotorized winter travelers. Now put those hands together for a thundering round of applause for the State Parks and their efforts to groom a 7-mile-long section of the Iron Horse Trail near Snoqualmie Pass. Applause also goes to the Cle Elum and Naches Ranger Districts, where there have been continued efforts to improve existing areas and add new trails for skiers.

Despite improvements, cross-country skiers still have only a small percentage of the available areas in the Cascades they can call their own. More and more of the main roads throughout the forests are becoming groomed

Skiers on Keechelus Ridge (Tour 7)

snowmobile speedways, which are noisy, smelly, and unsafe for slow-moving skiers. Although numerically cross-country skiers represent a much larger group than snowmobilers, only a fraction of the forest has been designated as safe areas for skis. To ask that a third of all forest roads be set aside for skiers and other self-propelled users would not be unreasonable.

Whether or not more roads are set aside for nonmotorized winter use is an issue that rests solely with us, the cross-country skiers. It is our responsibility to protect the areas reserved for self-propelled use and work to gain more areas. This is not an easy task for individual skiers to perform. Snowmobilers are a well-organized group with lobbyists, representatives, and a lot of money. Skiers are not.

There is a way to get involved in protecting our winter wonderland—write letters. Write letters to let the Forest Service and State Parks Commission know that you are interested in self-propelled winter recreation, that you are interested in preserving the areas that are currently reserved for the self-propelled, and that you would like to see more areas set aside for nonmotorized winter recreation. If meeting a snowmobile on your tour spoils your day, write about it. If skiing on a road groomed for snowmobiles is not enjoyable, write about it. If you were buzzed by snowmobiles while eating lunch, write about it. In your letter, note the area in which you were skiing, then briefly describe the incident or why you would have enjoyed the tour more if you hadn't had to share it with machines.

Here are some important addresses that will help you direct your letters to the correct agencies. Write to the Forest Supervisors:

Mount Baker–Snoqualmie
National Forest
Supervisors Office
21905 64th Avenue West
Mountlake Terrace, WA 98043

Wenatchee National Forest
P.O. Box 811
Wenatchee, WA 98801

Okanogan National Forest
Okanogan, WA 98840

Gifford Pinchot National Forest
500 West 12th Street
Vancouver, WA 98660

Olympic National Forest
Federal Building
Olympia, WA 98501

If you wish to write regarding the state parks, the address is:

Washington State Parks and Recreation Commission
7150 Cleanwater Lane KY-11
P.O. Box 42650
Olympia, WA 98504-2650

As no publication dealing with skiers' concerns exists, we find Pack and Paddle Magazine to be the best means available for passing information, sharing concerns, initiating letter-writing campaigns, and communicating with other skiers. Subscriptions can be obtained by writing to: Pack and Paddle, P.O. Box 1063, Port Orchard, WA 98366.

Guaranteeing our winter wonderland will not be a quick or an easy process. But if the Forest Service and the Parks Department know that we skiers are concerned with protecting and expanding our access into the forests and that any action depriving us of this very limited resource will be answered by a flood of protest, we will have gone a long way toward writing our own guarantee.

A NOTE ABOUT SAFETY

Safety is an important concern in all outdoor activities. No guidebook can alert you to every hazard or anticipate the limitations of every reader. Therefore, the descriptions of roads, trails, routes, and natural features in this book are not representations that a particular place or excursion will be safe for your party. When you follow any of the routes described in this book, you assume responsibility for your own safety. Under normal conditions, such excursions require the usual attention to traffic, road and trail conditions, weather, terrain, the capabilities of your party, and other factors. Keeping informed on current conditions and exercising common sense are the keys to a safe, enjoyable outing.

The Mountaineers

Backcountry skiing at Snoqualmie Pass (Tour 4)

INTRODUCTION

Washington's Cascade and Olympic Mountains provide infinite opportunity for excellent cross-country skiing, whether on groomed trails along peaceful valley floors, on scenic logging roads, or on open slopes of dormant volcanoes that cry out to be telemarked. This book is just an introduction to the vast amount of skiing that can be found. Particular emphasis has been given to the needs of the beginning and intermediate skier, but trails and routes have been included that will test the backcountry skier and challenge the mountaineer.

To repeat the caution that any guidebook must offer—especially one that deals in so undependable a substance as snow—the reader must keep in mind the publication date of this book. If he skis onto the scene a couple of years later, he must understand that the authors have no control over (1) the building of new roads or washing out of old ones, (2) the rules and regulations of government agencies, and (3) the falling down of trees and the piling up (or not piling up) of snow. In a word: Conditions are never the same twice, so be flexible in your plans.

HEADING OUT INTO WINTER

This book does not explain *how* to ski, just *where*. However, some tips are offered to help orient skiers toward wintertime fun. Further information can be found in Suggested Reading.

BE FLEXIBLE

During research for this book, many Ranger Districts and ski patrols were interviewed and one point was stressed: Be flexible. Have an alternate, safer trip plan if weather changes to create a high avalanche potential in your favorite area. If your second choice is also unsafe, plan a walk along a beach or to the city park. Your exercise of good judgment will help Ranger Districts and ski areas avoid the necessity of total winter closure for *all* users in order to protect a few thoughtless ones from their own stupidity.

SNO-PARKS

Many of the tours in this book start from Sno-Parks. These are designated parking areas plowed throughout the winter for recreation. Permits are required to park in these areas, and the fees are used to keep the parking sites plowed, bathrooms open, and trails maintained. Cars parking without permits can count on a ticket and possible towing. Sno-Park permits are sold by the day, week, or season. Before you head out, be sure and check the

Access section of your chosen tour to determine whether or not you will need a permit.

Permits are available at many outdoor equipment retail stores or by mail from: Washington State Parks and Recreation Commission, 7150 Cleanwater Lane KY-11, P.O. Box 42650, Olympia, WA 98504-2650.

HUTS AND WINTER CAMPING

What could be more fun than spending a night out in a snow-covered meadow, warm and cozy, with family or good friends. Thanks to the efforts of the Mt. Tahoma Trails Association, we now have some magnificent huts to enjoy. Of course, the hardy have endless choices for tent camping.

Huts

The Mt. Tahoma Trails Association has done wonderful work in creating nonmotorized access to the miles of logging roads above the Nisqually River valley. More than just access, they have built a system of public huts for skiers, a first for the state of Washington.

A Sno-Park permit is the only requirement to ski the Mt. Tahoma Trails, which criss-cross between DNR (Department of Natural Resources), Forest Service, National Park, and Champion (a private timber company) lands.

Advanced reservations, a very minimal processing fee, and a damage deposit are all that is required to stay at one of the scenically located huts. For a Hut Reservation Form, send a self-addressed stamped envelope to: Mt. Tahoma Trails Association, Attn: Hut Reservation Program, P.O. Box 206, Ashford, WA 98304. Please note that despite the fact that the huts were funded with Sno-Park money, association members get first choice at hut reservations.

The Mt. Tahoma Trails Association is a completely volunteer organization with a lot of enthusiasm and very little in the way of funds. The association would welcome your membership and support. Volunteers for the ski patrol are also needed.

Winter Camping

Most Forest Service campgrounds are closed in winter by snow. However, some state parks remain open, with plowed access roads and one or two campsites and offering the added attraction of heated restrooms.

When winter camping takes you away from established campgrounds, set camp wherever you feel safe. Avoid pitching a tent under trees heavy with snow; when least expected (day or night), "mushrooms" may fall from above and crush your tent.

Whether in the backcountry or on groomed tracks of a resort, carry out your garbage. (If you packed it in full, you can pack it out empty.) Burying leftovers under a few inches of snow only hides them until the spring melt.

A snowy afternoon in the tent on a winter camping trip

Also be careful with human waste. Hidden beneath the snow may be a stream or a summer hiking trail.

Water can be difficult to come by in winter. Most small streams are either hidden beneath the snow or flowing in grand white canyons too steep to descend. If day-skiing, carry water. On a trip lasting overnight or longer, carry a long string for lowering a bucket to an open stream as well as a stove and enough fuel to melt snow. Even in winter, the water from streams in areas where people and/or beavers and other such critters live in summer should be boiled or filtered.

When spending the day or several days out skiing, take care where you park your car. A sudden winter storm can make bare and dry logging roads deep in white and impossible to drive, leaving your car stranded—maybe until the spring melt. Always travel with a shovel in the car and a watchful eye on the weather.

WHAT TO TAKE

Every skier who ventures more than a few feet away from the car should be prepared to spend the night out. Winter storms can come with great speed and force, creating whiteouts that leave the skier with nowhere to go. Each ski pack must include the Ten Essentials, plus one:

1. Extra clothing—more than needed in the worst of weather. (See More Words Concerning Clothing, below.)
2. Extra food and water—there should be some left over at the end of the trip.
3. Sunglasses—a few hours of bright sun on snow can cause a pounding headache or temporary blindness.
4. Knife—for first aid and emergency repairs.
5. First-aid kit—just in case.
6. Fire starter—chemical starter to get wet wood burning.
7. Waterproof matches in a waterproof container with a striker that you have tested before you leave home—to start a fire.
8. Flashlight—be sure to have extra batteries as well as an extra bulb.
9. Map—make sure it's the right one for the trip.
10. Compass—keep in mind the declination.

Plus: Repair kit—including a spare ski tip, spare screws and binding bail (if changeable), heavy-duty tape, and a combination wrench–pliers–screwdriver.

Other items to carry may include a small shovel, sun cream, and a large plastic tarp to use as a "picnic blanket" or for emergency shelter. All these items should fit comfortably into a day pack. Obviously, a fanny pack will not hold all the listed items. Fanny packs are strictly for track and resort skiing where one is carrying only a sandwich and a few waxes.

MORE WORDS CONCERNING CLOTHING

There is no dress code for cross-country skiing. Clothing can be anything from high-fashion Lycra to mismatched army surplus. However, many of the garments sold for cross-country skiing are designed for resort skiing or racing, providing flexibility and style, but not much warmth.

In the wilderness, warmth is crucial. Covering your body from head to toe in synthetic long underwear, or wool if you like to itch, and using two or more layers on the upper body to regulate heating ensure a pleasant journey rather than a bone-chilling ordeal. So go ahead and wear that designer outfit, but be sure and have a layer of long underwear underneath and another layer with you that can be put on over it.

Rain gear is essential. Rain pants and jackets made of coated nylon or breathable waterproof material work best for warmth, dryness, and flexibility.

SKIS AND BOOTS

What length of ski to buy, with side-cut or without, with metal edges or without, hard or soft camber? What boots are best, flexible or stiff? These and many more questions could fill a book—and they do. Our one and only suggestion is to purchase a waxless ski as your first pair. Learning to ski can be complicated enough without the frustration of trying to wax for the ever-changing snow conditions of the Cascade and Olympic Mountains. When looking for that new pair of skis, avoid stores that just happen to have a few cross-country skis in stock. Stores that have special cross-country departments and employees who enjoy cross-country skiing will be able to give you a better understanding of what you need and what you don't.

Cross-country boots come in two varieties, lightweight for track skiing and light touring and heavyweight for backcountry and telemark skiing. The type of boots you have will determine the type of bindings you need, so buy the boots first.

TECHNIQUE

Cross-country skiing looks simple enough, but proper technique is very important to ensure a good time. Even expert downhillers have problems the first day on cross-country skis. The narrowness, flexible bindings, and softness of the shoes give an entirely different feeling. Books are helpful, but one or two lessons may be needed. Many organizations offer a two-lesson plan, the first to get you started in the right direction and the second to correct any problems you have.

PETS

Although in some jurisdictions the family pet is permitted to tag along on summer hikes, wintertime should be left to the two-legged family members. Skiing through knee-deep powder is lots of fun, but not for the ski-less family pet, floundering in a white morass. Pets also tend to destroy ski tracks by leaving behind deep paw prints and brown klister.

Pets are not allowed in National Parks or on any groomed ski trails.

GUIDE TO THE GUIDEBOOK

This section provides a brief explanation of the terms used in the Information Blocks preceding each tour description. It also explains how to best use the information in this book and what some of the commonly employed terms mean in non-skier English.

CLASS (CLASSIFICATION)

To help you choose a tour we have noted one of three different trail classifications at the beginning of each Information Block. You will find a more complete explanation of the trail conditions in the following text.

Groomed: These are skier-only trails that have been smoothed out by a machine to provide the best possible skiing conditions. You will find several types of grooming; the simplest is snow compacted by a snowmobile on a regular basis. Many groomed trails are set with machine-made tracks for your skis. Groomed trails may also include a skating lane. No dogs are allowed on groomed trails. Many of these trails require the paying of a day-use fee.

Self-Propelled: These are areas closed to snowmobiles. You may have the company of snowshoers and hikers on your tour.

Multiple Use: These are tours on roads or trails that must be shared with snowmobiles and possibly even four-wheel-drive trucks.

RATING

Each tour has been rated for difficulty based on the amount of skill required to enjoy the trip. The rating is located in the Information Block at the head of the tour's description. For the sake of simplicity we have used five categories that tend to be broad and somewhat overlapping; consider them to be merely suggestions.

Easiest: No skill requirement. Anyone can have fun the very first time on skis and families will find these great places for very small children. These are also areas where sleds loaded with gear or children can be pulled with relative ease. These tours generally are in open meadows, valley bottoms, level logging roads, or abandoned railroad grades.

More Difficult: The minimum skills required are good balance, kick and glide, and simple stopping techniques such as pole dragging, snowplowing, and sitting down—and a good sense of humor. The tours at this level are generally on logging roads, marked Forest Service loops, or prepared tracks, and will cover some steep terrain.

Most Difficult: Tours with this designation may be long, very steep, or both. Skiers who attempt these tours should have endurance and the ability to descend steep slopes in all types of snow conditions. Minimum required skills include the kick-turn, herringbone, and snowplow turn. Skiers who can telemark will enjoy these tours more than those who cannot. These tours are generally on narrow, steep logging roads and may have optional off-road side trips and descent routes.

Backcountry: The minimum skills required for these tours are full control of skis at all times, mastery of the telemark or any turn, and the ability to stop quickly. Some backcountry tours require basic routefinding to navigate summer hiking trails and cross-country routes.

Mountaineer: In addition to backcountry skiing skills, mountaineer trips require competence in routefinding and knowledge of snow and avalanche conditions, glacier travel techniques, weather savvy, winter camping skills, winter survival skills, and mountaineering skills.

ROUND TRIP

Snow levels vary from year to year and from day to day. Therefore, the starting point of your tour, especially on logging roads, may vary. A base point (which may or may not be your actual starting point) has been assigned and is found in each tour's Access section; the trailhead elevation and skiing time are figured from this point.

SKIING TIME

This is the time spent skiing to and from the destination and does *not* include lunch or rest stops. The times are calculated from the tour's base point. If the snowline is above this point, plan less time; if below, plan more. The times given for each trail assume good conditions. If a track must be broken through heavy snow or the surface is extremely hard ice, add a generous amount of extra time.

In some cases the number of miles and amount of skiing time given are variable. These trails are generally over logging roads where snow level suggests different starting points and destinations in winter and spring.

ELEVATION GAIN

This entry simply helps you determine the amount of climbing you must do between the parking lot and your destination. Ups and downs have been calculated into the total elevation gain.

HIGH POINT

This entry notes the highest point you will reach on your tour. You will find the high point an important piece of information when the snow level is either fluctuating wildly or when the winter has been unseasonably warm and you are trying to guess if you will find any snow at all.

BEST

"Best" is an attempt to answer the unanswerable. When is the "best" time to do the tour? The times we provided are guesses based on an average year. However, as any long-time skier can tell you, there is no such thing as an "average" snow year in Washington's Cascade or Olympic Mountains. Some years skiing must be done at 5,000 feet or above; other years skiing is good through June at 3,000 feet; some years the skiing is superb on Seattle's golf courses for most of January.

In an attempt to say when skiing is best for each trail, certain generalizations have been made about that mythical average snow year. The time band given is a narrow one. Skiing often starts as much as a month before given times and lasts a month after. Some winters skiing may not be possible on trails below 4,000 feet. If in doubt, call the area Ranger Station, listen to pass reports, or contact local mountain shops before starting out.

AVALANCHE POTENTIAL

Tours in this book have been selected for their safety in winter and no known areas of extreme hazard have been included. The warnings given here are about areas to avoid at times when the snow is unstable. To know when these times are, skiers must make it their responsibility to inform themselves about current weather and snow conditions. The best source for up-to-date information on the weather and avalanche conditions in the Washington Cascades and Olympics is a weather radio with continuous reports from the NOAA (National Oceanic and Atmospheric Administration). For specific tours call the Ranger Station in that district; on weekends there will be a recorded message.

Your best defense against avalanches is knowledge. Check Suggested Reading for detailed discussions. Several things to particularly watch for are as follows:

- Avalanche danger is especially high during warming trends or after a heavy snowfall; at these times avoid leeward slopes and travel on ridge tops.
- Steep hillsides, particularly north-facing, receive their first dose of sun for many months in the spring. After being stable all winter, these slopes may be covered by spring, or climax, avalanches.
- Wind causes snow to build up on the leeward side of ridges, creating dangerous overhangs called cornices. Use caution when approaching a ridge top—you may walk out atop a cornice with empty air beneath. A good rule is never to ski beyond the line of trees or snowblown rocks that mark the true crest of a ridge. It is equally dangerous to ski under a cornice as over it. Cornices may break off and trigger avalanches below.

Forecasting agencies express the daily hazard in the following four classifications:

1. Low Avalanche Hazard—mostly stable snow.
2. Moderate Avalanche Hazard—areas of unstable snow on steep, open slopes or gullies.
3. High Avalanche Hazard—snow pack very unstable. Avalanches highly probable on steep slopes and in gullies.
4. Extreme Avalanche Hazard—travel in the mountains unsafe. Better to head for the beach.

These classifications of hazard have to do with the weather's contribution to the avalanches. Each trail in this book has been rated as to the potential of the terrain for avalanches. The two factors of hazard and potential must be put together by the skier to make an accurate judgment of the situation.

If the avalanche *potential* for the trail is listed as **none**, the trail may be safely skied on days when the *hazard* is low, moderate, or high.

Areas with **low** avalanche *potential* normally may be skied on days when the *hazard* is low or moderate.

A **moderate** avalanche *potential* indicates the area is always to be skied with caution and then only when the *hazard* is low.

Avalanche forecasting is not an exact science. As when driving a car, one has to accept a certain amount of risk and use the forecast as a guide, not as a certainty. It is important always to seek up-to-date avalanche information before each trip, even for trips of **low** to **moderate** avalanche *potential.*

MAPS

Blankets of snow add new difficulties to routefinding. Signs are covered, road junctions are obscured, and trails blend into the surrounding countryside. Never start out without a good map of the area to be skied.

To help you find the best map for your tour, we have recommended a topographic map (USGS, Green Trails, Custom Correct, or USFS) in each tour description. The USGS maps are published by the United States Geological Survey. These maps cover the entire country and are unequaled for off-road and off-trail routefinding. Unfortunately, USGS maps are not kept up-to-date in terms of roads and trails. The Green Trails maps are published in Washington and updated with some regularity; however, these maps do not cover areas beyond the heartland of the Cascades and Olympics.

Custom Correct maps cover only the Olympic Mountains. Unlike Green Trails, these maps do not follow the USGS established grids. Instead, Custom Correct maps cover a usage area, creating a series of maps that overlap each other. To date, Custom Correct maps have the best record of keeping current with the road and trail changes in the Olympics.

The USFS (United States Forest Service) Ranger District maps cover an entire Ranger District showing contours, roads, and trails. These are outstanding maps and sold at a bargain price. Unfortunately the maps are huge and tear easily. They are generally the most up-to-date maps available.

Both the USGS and Green Trails maps are available at outdoor equipment stores and many Forest Service Ranger Stations. The USFS Ranger District maps are available only through the Forest Service and may be purchased in person or by mail-order from the Ranger District offices or from the Forest Headquarters office.

Another excellent resource is an up-to-date Forest Service Recreation Map, available for a small fee at Ranger Stations (on weekdays) or by writing the district offices.

1 BANDERA OVERLOOK

Class: *multiple use*
Rating: *more difficult*
Round trip: *7 miles*
Skiing time: *3 hours*
Elevation gain: *885 feet*

High point: *2,485 feet*
Best: *January*
Avalanche potential: *low*
Map: *Green Trails, Bandera No. 206*

When the snow level descends from mountain passes to the lowlands of Puget Sound, when the interstate highways serve as championship skating rinks, the Bandera Overlook becomes a very popular tour. The overlook is actually a trailhead parking area overlooking the South Fork Snoqualmie River valley. From river and freeway and snow-covered valley the eye rises to a skyline of ridges and peaks. When the snow level jumps back up to the lofty heights, you may have the area to yourself, if there is any snow, or you may head off on the neighboring Mason Lake Way.

Skiing near Bandera Overlook

Access: Drive Interstate 90 east from North Bend 14.9 miles to Exit 45. Park only in the plowed area on the south or north side of the freeway. Do not park in the interchange area (1,680 feet).

The Tour: Following signs to Lookout Road, cross to the north side of Interstate 90 to find a paved forest road. The first mile of the tour parallels the freeway. When the road divides, go right on Road 9030, which is signed to Talapus Lake Trail. (Straight ahead is Mason Lake Way, which does not go to the lake but is a good tour in February.)

The road climbs steadily passing recent logging operations but never

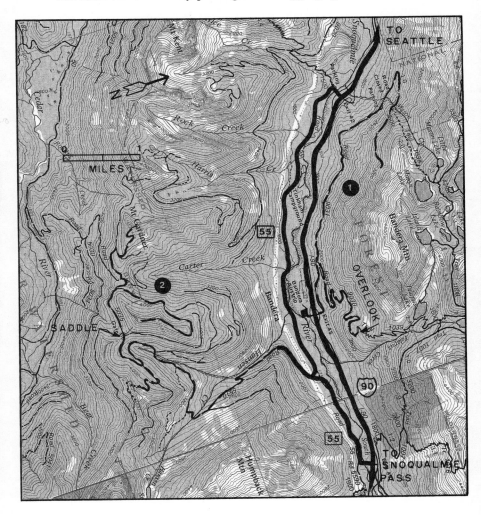

leaving the heavy forest cover. Climbing higher you will eventually see Mount Gardner and a frozen-looking McClellan Butte to the southwest poking over the tree tops. At 2 miles Granite Mountain appears to the northeast. The road ends at the overlook at 3½ miles. This nice level picnic spot is the Talapus Lake Trailhead. If time remains after trying to name all the peaks and drainages from McClellan Butte to the backside of the Snoqualmie Pass Ski Areas, ski up the trail for ¼ mile just for the fun of cruising down through the trees.

When the snow level is higher than Interstate 90, drive as far as possible up Mason Lake Way, then ski the road to the open slopes under Bandera Mountain, with views rivaling those from the overlook.

---

2 HANSEN CREEK

Class: *multiple use*
Rating: *most difficult*
Round trip: *2–15 miles*
Skiing time: *2–8 hours*
Elevation gain: *up to 2,693 feet*

High point: *4,693 feet*
Best: *March–May*
Avalanche potential: *low*
Map: *Green Trails, Bandera No. 206*

Map on page 23

Throughout the winter the Hansen Creek area is inaccessible for all practical purposes, due to the lack of parking and high avalanche potential. In spring, however, there are valleys, ridge tops, clearcuts, and miles of logging roads to explore on skis—and miles and miles of snow-covered mountains to look at.

Access: Drive Interstate 90 east from North Bend to Exit 47. Turn right (west) on Asahel Curtis–Tinkham Road for 0.2 mile to a T intersection and the end of pavement. Take the right fork. After 1.3 miles turn left on Hansen Creek Road No. 5510. Follow it as it climbs steadily west 0.8 mile, then park in a wide turnout on the left (2,000 feet). Obviously, if there is not enough snow here, continue on up.

The Tour: From the parking area the road turns abruptly south, entering Hansen Creek Valley and crossing under a tall, spindly train trestle. At just over 1 mile pass a spur to the left and, in a long ½ mile more, a second spur. Beyond the second intersection the road levels off in the upper valley and enters clearcuts. Views begin, starting with Bandera Mountain to the north. Stay on the main road as it crosses Hansen Creek at 2 miles (2,900 feet) then

Open slopes in the upper Hansen Creek drainage

swings onto a side valley where Granite Mountain appears to the east of Bandera. At 3 miles cross an unnamed tributary of Hansen Creek and reach a major junction. Take the left fork, heading up the valley. From this point you have a choice of objectives.

The most popular objective is the saddle at the upper end of the valley. To reach the saddle, follow the road as it curves left around the valley, then take the logging road on the right. The road climbs to the 3,900-foot ridge top at 5½ miles. From the saddle you have an excellent view over the forbidden lands of the Cedar River Valley, source of Seattle's water.

If you are still feeling energetic, you can head either north or south from the saddle. If you head south for 2 miles you'll reach a 4,693-foot knoll with views of Mount Rainier, Cedar River, and McClellan Butte. On your way back, practice a few turns in one of the many clearcuts.

North from the saddle the road provides views over the South Fork Snoqualmie, from the ribbonlike freeway in the valley up to rugged summits of Snoqualmie Pass peaks. At 1½ miles beyond the saddle, the road ends at a viewpoint of Mount Gardner, Bandera Mountain, and Mount Defiance.

3 THE IRON HORSE TRAIL

Class: *groomed*
Rating: *easiest*
Round trip: *up to 14½ miles*
Skiing time: *up to 6 hours*
Elevation gain: *70 feet*

High point: *2,540 feet*
Best: *mid-December–February*
Avalanche potential: *high*
Map: *Green Trails, Snoqualmie Pass No. 207*

A nearly level tour? Perfect for beginners and young families? Yes!!!

For this rare gem of a tour we can thank the hard-working Rails-to-Trails program, whose energetic pursuit of the abandoned Milwaukee Railroad Grade has saved it from the hands of greedy land grabbers and preserved this national treasure for recreational use. At this time the 7½-mile section of the old railroad grade on the east side of Snoqualmie Pass between Hyak and the Stampede Pass Road is groomed and reserved for skiers' use during the winter months.

This section of the railroad grade is particularly scenic, and skiers will find sections of quiet forest as well as open views of Kendall Knob, Gold Creek valley, Chikamin Ridge, and Mount Catherine from the shores of Keechelus Lake.

The railroad grade provides an almost level tour, and the state park provides a double set of groomed ski tracks, which are ideal for practicing the

Iron Horse Trail near Stampede Pass Road

long, gliding, diagonal stride of the traditional skier while the open area between the tracks allows for the high-speed, leg-stretching skate of the nouveau skier.

The railroad grade has many possible turnaround points for round-trip skiers or, with a car shuttle, you can arrange a 7-mile, one-way tour to the Eastbound Price Creek Sno-Park on Interstate 90.

Access: Drive Interstate 90 east from Snoqualmie Pass summit to Hyak/Rocky Run Exit 54. Following the boat ramp signs, go left at the Hyak Ski Area entrance and follow a narrow road that parallels Interstate 90 for 0.5 mile. Just before the Department of Transportation complex, go right. After 0.7 mile you will arrive at the Keechelus Lake–Iron Horse State Park Sno-Park parking area and outhouse located on the right-hand side of the road (2,540 feet). If making a one-way trip, leave your second vehicle at the East-bound Price Creek Sno-Park (see Tour 9 for driving directions).

The Tour: The tour begins on the west side of the parking area and follows the well-maintained railroad grade south. This is a popular tour and you will be sharing the tracks with all types of skiers from beginners to experts, ages 2 to 95 years old.

The railroad grade starts off by paralleling the access road, which continues on from the Sno-Park for another ⅛ mile to the winter play area at the boat launch. Young skiers in particular will watch the sledding and inner-tube riding with undisguised envy. The railroad grade then

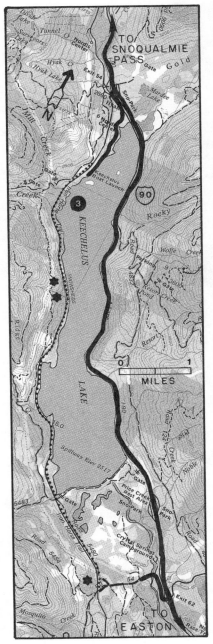

View over Keechelus Lake from the Iron Horse Trail

leaves the lakeshore and swings through a forested cove to cross first Mill Creek then Cold Creek at 1¼ miles. The tour continues through the trees for another ½ mile then returns to the lakeshore.

At 2¼ miles the railroad grade passes under a cliff, a very dangerous area when the snow is unstable. When the trains used to travel this route, they were sheltered here by two snowsheds. Old woodwork from the sheds can still be seen on the hillside above. A large red sign warns you of the danger before you enter this area. Use considerable caution and do not linger when passing through this hazardous area. The avalanche area lasts for ¼ mile, after which the tour is once again relatively avalanche-free.

The railroad grade parallels the lake for a time then plows across a small peninsula before returning to the lakeshore. At 4 miles you will cross the Roaring Creek bridge. Continue south, dodging in and out of the trees with occasional views until at 5½ miles you cross Meadow Creek and soon after arrive at an intersection. To the left lies the Keechelus Lake dam, a great place for a sunny-day picnic and the ideal turnaround point if you are heading back to the north end of the lake. This is also the place where you must leave the railroad grade if you are doing a one-way trip.

The railroad grade crosses the Meadow Creek Road and continues south. The road and railroad grade are close together in this section, and there is a constant roar of snowmobiles on the road below, shredding the quiet peace of winter. A second avalanche shoot is crossed at 6¾ miles. When the avalanche hazard is high it is best to descend to the road to cross this section, then return to the railroad grade for the final ½ mile.

At 7¼ mile the railroad grade crosses the Stampede Pass Road. Iron Horse State Park continues on to the town of Easton; however, from this point on the railroad grade is open to speeding snowmobiles and rather unpleasant to ski.

If you are making a one-way trip, leave the railroad grade at Meadow Creek and ski out to the dam. You will pass a snow-covered gate then follow the road right along the top of the dam. At the far side of the dam, note the maintenance buildings in a clearing below. Using a handy, but somewhat steep ramp, descend from the dam then ski along the left side of the buildings.

After passing the buildings find a narrow road that heads straight into the forest, paralleling a line of telephone poles. The road leads to a meadow where you will find a trail on your left marked by blue diamonds. Follow the markers to a bridge over a creek then head right and climb up a short, steep hill. At the top go left for 50 feet to end your tour at the Eastbound Price Creek Sno-Park.

I-90 CORRIDOR

MOUNT CATHERINE LOOP

Class: groomed
Rating: backcountry
Loop trip: 10½ miles
Skiing time: 6 hours
Elevation gain: 1,520 feet

High point: 4,060 feet
Best: mid-December–April
Avalanche potential: low
Map: Green Trails, Snoqualmie Pass No. 207

Map on page 30

Not long ago cross-country skiers were stereotyped as long-haired hippies, who smelled of pine tar and wet wool and used bamboo ski poles that left peace-sign imprints in the snow. Those "granola" skiers used to drive to Snoqualmie Pass, park with the downhill skiers, then head out to the uncharted forest behind the ski areas.

Today the uncharted forests of the past have been replaced by groomed ski trails with two sets of machine-made tracks for classic skiers and a wide lane for skaters in the middle. This is a marvelous place to witness how modern technology has transformed the sport. The granola skiers have shed their natural skin for one of plastic: skis, poles, boots, and even clothing.

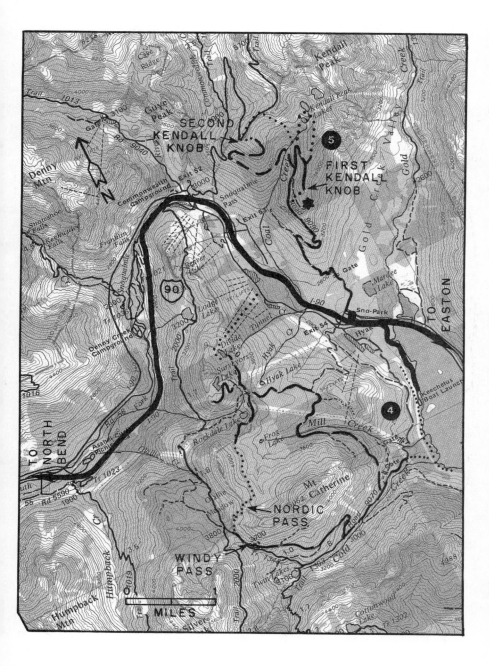

Thanks to The Mountaineers and the Sierra Club, as well as cheerful co-operation from the Ski Acres Nordic Center, backcountry skiers can still access their traditional telemarking grounds and complete the ever-popular loop around Mount Catherine. This is a difficult route that is partially on groomed trails and partially on steep, forested hillsides.

Skiers on the Mount Catherine Loop

Access: Following the directions given in Tour 3, drive to the Keechelus Lake–Iron Horse State Park Sno-Park (2,540 feet).

The Tour: From the parking area ski south on the groomed railroad grade. After a level, and very easy, ¾ mile the railroad grade crosses first Mill Creek then a second, small, unnamed creek. After crossing the second creek look for a convenient way to descend off the railroad grade on your right. Once down, head to a band of trees and look for a blue diamond trail marker. (The sign for this junction is subject to vandalism and may or may not be present.)

The trail climbs a narrow forested path up the creek valley for ⅛ mile then bends right to intersect the groomed ski tracks on Road 9070 at 1 mile. Go left and ski up the "Common Corridor." Please observe all the courtesies of skiing on groomed tracks.

The road dips, crosses Mill Creek (2,660 feet), then begins to climb. At 1¾ miles reach a well-signed intersection and a choice. When the snow is icy or crusty you should head right and ski up the Hidden Valley Trail, doing the steepest portion of the loop first. On the rare days when the snow is somewhat soft, reverse the loop and have a blast on the steep descents.

Head up the Hidden Valley Road climbing steeply to an outstanding viewpoint (3,200 feet) over Keechelus Lake, Mount Margaret, and Keechelus Ridge at 2½ miles. Continue to follow the road, which heads into a nearly level contour across the clearcut hillside above Mill Creek. At 3½ miles the road begins to climb again and the Common Corridor ends. At this point you must go left, leaving the groomed ski trails in favor of breaking your own trail across the open clearcuts. The easiest and most direct route is to head to your left and follow the drainage up to tiny Frog Lake (3,570 feet) then head west, up the forested hillside, to intersect the Hyak Lake Trail (3,830 feet). The alternate route is to parallel the groomed trails up two humps to find the trail maintained by The Mountaineers and the Sierra Club. This trail is well marked but can be difficult to negotiate through the trees when there is not a lot of snow.

Once you are in the forest you will follow the old route of the Pacific Crest Trail on a steady ascent. The trail crosses the crest of a knoll then descends past a weather station before making the final climb at the 6-mile point to 4,060-foot Nordic Pass.

The descent from the pass is very steep and quite often side-slipped or walked. At the base of the steep slope lies 3,800-foot Windy Pass and a broad expanse of very telemarkable clearcuts, which extend west to the base of Silver Peak and north to excellent views of Granite Mountain. The groomed trails that criss-cross this area are private and must be avoided.

From Windy Pass, head southeast down the groomed Common Corridor Road for 3 miles. Climb the short hill beyond Mill Creek to find your trail back to the railroad grade and the Iron Horse Sno-Park at 9½ miles. Go right and descend this difficult trail back to the railroad grade to reach your starting point at 10½ miles.

5 KENDALL—KNOBS, LAKES, AND LOOPS

Class: *self-propelled*
Rating: *more difficult*
Round trip: *7 miles*
Skiing time: *4 hours*
Elevation gain: *1,700 feet*

High point: *4,400 feet*
Best: *December–April*
Avalanche potential: *moderate*
Map: *Green Trails, Snoqualmie Pass No. 207*

Map on page 30

Open slopes, grand views, and small forested lakes are just some of the features of this vast area below Kendall Peak. This is the kind of area that has something for everyone from the smallest child to the hardiest backcountry skier. Nordic outcasts can leave their snowboarding and downhilling friends and family at the chairlifts and head across the valley for a day of exercise and fun then pick them up from the resort on the way home. Arrive early to secure a parking spot, and be prepared for a lot of company.

Watching the downhill skiers across the valley from the road up Kendall Knob

33

The fate of this area is uncertain. Developers intending to build vacation houses in Gold Creek valley wish to eliminate the Sno-Park and all skier access to the area. We hope that skier outrage will convince the Forest Service and the State Parks Department to find a way to keep this area open. If you would like to help save public parking at Snoqualmie Pass, please write a letter to the North Bend District Ranger, 42404 SE North Bend Way, North Bend, WA 98045, and to the Washington State Parks and Recreation Commission, 7150 Cleanwater Lane KY-11, P.O. Box 42650, Olympia, WA 98504-2650.

Access: Drive Interstate 90 east from Snoqualmie Pass 2 miles to Hyak/Rocky Run Exit 54. Park in the Gold Creek Sno-Park on the north side of the freeway along the plowed section of the old highway (2,640 feet). From the Sno-Park pick one of three possible destinations.

First Kendall Knob: This tour heads north up Gold Creek valley on level road. At ⅛ mile the road turns uphill and climbs quite steeply. At ½ mile the road forks; stay left and switchback up through an old clearcut. Two major spur roads are passed, the first on the right and the second on the left, as your road heads into the first of two steep switchbacks where the views start to get exciting. A third spur is passed on the left as you begin to switchback. At 2 miles (3,600 feet) the road heads north through trees then across an old clearcut with excellent views of the skiers on the slopes at Ski Acres. Pass a spur road on the left then a road on the right as you head up into a fold of the hill. At 3¼ miles the road divides at a switchback; go right and continue climbing until the road reaches a narrow saddle on a ridge. Go right and ski to the road's end on a flat landing atop the 4,400-foot summit of the knob.

Kendall Peak Lakes: The lakes offer a peaceful backcountry escape as well as an outstanding run down through the trees. This route has a *backcountry* rating.

Following the First Kendall Knob route, ski 3¾ miles to the narrow saddle on the ridge directly below First Kendall Knob. Go left and climb up over two short rises. At the top of the second rise, leave the road and head left into the trees and traverse north to a stream drainage. Turn uphill and follow the stream to the lowest lake (4,300 feet), a short ½ mile above Kendall Knob. The second lake lies another ¼ mile up the valley. This is the turn-around point, as serious avalanche hazard lies beyond.

For the return trip, ski straight down the valley from the lakes to intersect the road leading to the knob. Widely spaced trees provide telemarkers with fun obstacles to negotiate and the snow remains powdery long after the exposed slopes turn to mush.

Second Kendall Knob: This 10-mile round trip has the best telemarking in the area and views galore. To the south you will look over the white blanket covering Keechelus Lake. In the western skies rise Meadow Mountain, Tinkham Peak, and Mount Rainier. Silver Peak, Mount Catherine, and all the ski resorts of Snoqualmie Pass lie right beneath your feet. To the north Guye Peak, Denny Mountain, The Tooth, Bryant Peak, and Chair Peak pierce the sky. And to the east sits the Alpine Lakes Wilderness Area with its enclave of protected trees terminating at the buttresslike walls of Kendall Peak.

Ski up the road to First Kendall Knob for 3⅛ miles. At this point you will have passed the switchbacks, skied through the forest, crossed the old clearcut, and traversed a recent clearcut slope to a point where a steep hill rises on the left. Shortly beyond, a road takes off on the right and then another road branches off to the left. Take the left-hand road, and ski across the clearcut. You will descend slightly to cross Coal Creek then climb again. The road ends in an open basin near the top. Continue on, breaking your own trail for the final ¼ mile to the summit of the 4,720-foot knob.

For the descent, the slopes heading due west down from the summit are the most open and stable. The slopes on the south side are steep and rocky and should only be skied in very stable conditions.

6 MOUNT MARGARET

Class: multiple use
Rating: backcountry
Round trip: 9 miles to false summit
Skiing time: 5 hours
Elevation gain: 2,880 feet
High point: 5,440 feet
Best: January–mid-April
Avalanche potential: moderate
Map: Green Trails, Snoqualmie Pass
  No. 207

Map on page 36

The west side of Mount Margaret offers open slopes that compare to the best downhill ski areas in length and variety. A day may be spent making challenging runs down the

Open slopes below the summit are excellent for telemarking

clearcut hillsides or climbing to the rugged ridge just below the summit of Mount Margaret to enjoy the extraordinary views.

Do not ski this tour after a heavy snowfall or rainstorm. Before the west side of the mountain was completely logged, Mount Margaret was considered a safe area for touring in almost any conditions. Now, with over 2,000 vertical feet of barren slopes, the section of this tour paralleling the freeway is potentially dangerous.

Access: Drive Interstate 90 east from Snoqualmie Pass to Hyak/Rocky Run Exit 54. Go left, under the freeway, to the north side and turn right at the Gold Creek Sno-Park. Drive 0.8 mile and park near the end of the plowed road (2,560 feet). This is still part of the Sno-Park area so be sure to have a permit.

The Tour: The first 2-mile section of this tour follows the old highway along the edge of the freeway and is admittedly a bore. There are great views of Keechelus Lake and obnoxious views of the freeway. After passing several summer homes, the road turns uphill and gets to the serious business of gaining elevation.

Near the end of the first mile of climbing, the road enters open clearcuts. An abrupt switchback at 3 miles is the scene of a possibly confusing intersection; stay right. At 3½ miles is another junction. The right fork descends gradually for 6 miles to the Kachess Lake Road. Take the left fork and climb steeply. Pass the summer parking lot for the Mount Margaret–Lake Lillian Trail (3,600 feet). After another 100 yards take a spur road on the left and head steeply uphill, following the summer route to Mount Margaret. Once

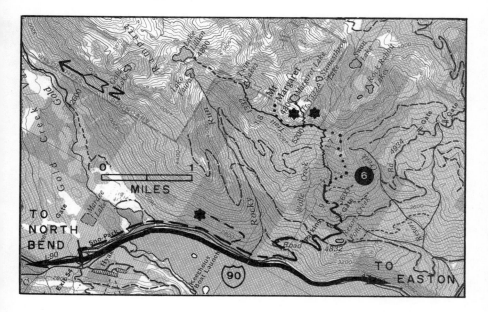

Lunch on the false summit of Mount Margaret; Mount Rainier in distance

over the initial steep climb look up to the top of the clearcuts. The objective is to reach the upper right corner of the clearcut hillside either on the road or across the slopes and not be totally distracted by the terrific views, featuring Mount Rainier and Keechelus Lake.

From the top of the clearcut follow a logging road to a higher clearcut. Continue on the road to the upper left corner of this clearcut and through a narrow band of trees overlooked by the loggers to a final clearcut and the road-end. Climb past ghost trees to the ridge top (4,800 feet), where whole new horizons extend south over miles of logged slopes to the Stampede Pass area. If your descending skills are not as strong as your climbing ability, this is a good place to turn around.

The rest of the climb is in timber. Follow the ridge crest when the going is easy, and drop over to the west side when the ridge is rough. Stay well away from the east edge—which is often corniced.

The final ascent is up partially forested slopes to the 5,440-foot false summit. Taking care to stay well back from the corniced edge, gaze to the dark granite massif of Mount Stuart. Bears Breast Mountain stands out among the Dutch Miller Gap Peaks. West and north are spiky peaks near Snoqualmie Pass.

The summit of Mount Margaret lies temptingly near and only 90 feet higher. But the route crosses steep slopes and giant cornices, so stay healthy and stay where you are. You can always come back and check it out in summer.

7 RELAY TOWER—KEECHELUS RIDGE

Round Trip

Class: *multiple use*
Rating: *backcountry*
Round trip: *8 miles*
Skiing time: *4 hours*
Elevation gain: *2,120 feet*
High point: *4,960 feet*
Best: *January–March*
Avalanche potential: *low*
Map: *Green Trails, Snoqualmie Pass No. 207*

Loop Trip

Class: *multiple use*
Rating: *most difficult*
Loop trip: *11½ miles*
Skiing time: *6 hours*
Elevation gain: *2,120 feet*
High point: *4,960 feet*
Best: *December–March*
Avalanche potential: *low*
Map: *Green Trails, Snoqualmie Pass No. 207*

If telemarking is your addiction, one of the best midwinter fixes in the Snoqualmie Pass area is found on the hillsides of Keechelus Ridge. If telemarking has not brought you ultimate joy, then ignore the questionable lure of the clearcuts and get set for one of the best logging road loops in the area. On one point both telemarkers and non-telemarkers can agree: The views on this loop are truly excellent.

Although this is a popular snowmobile area, after you leave the parking area you will see few machines until you reach the summit. Loop skiers will have to share their route on the descent. As always, a midweek getaway is the best way to avoid exhaust fumes.

Access: West-siders, drive Interstate 90 east from Snoqualmie Pass for 10 miles to Stampede Pass/Kachess Lake Exit 62. Turn left, cross the overpass, and return to the freeway, then head west for 1 mile to the Westbound Price Creek Sno-Park (2,560 feet).

East-siders will find the Sno-Park 1 mile past Exit 62. However, for the return trip you will have to drive 7 miles west to Hyak/Rocky Run Exit 54 before making the U-turn east.

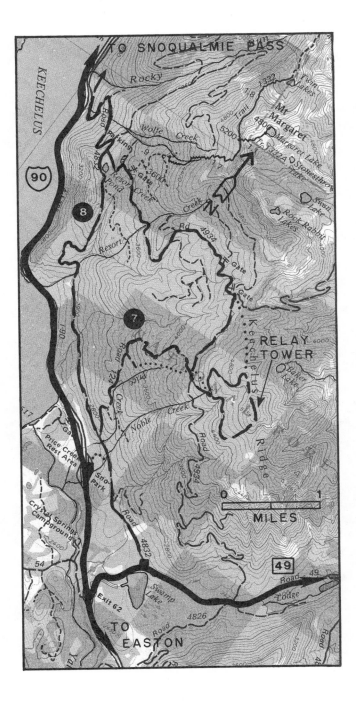

Round-trip Tour: Follow the signed snowmobile route from the Sno-Park for ½ mile to Forest Road 4832, a groomed snowmobile route. Go right on Road 4832 for 50 feet, then take a left on Road (4832)124. This road has one purpose and that is to climb, so get set and head up.

The road climbs along the upper edge of a clearcut and rounds a crew-cut hill. Price Creek is now on your right. As the hill on the left comes to an end you will find an unmarked and somewhat confusing intersection (at about 1 mile from the Sno-Park). Here you have a choice. You can continue left on the somewhat overgrown Road (4832)124 and follow it all the way to Road 4934, or you can slap on the climbing skins and take the narrow and somewhat overgrown road on the far right, which climbs south while Price Creek swings southeast. At 1½ miles watch for another abandoned road branching right and follow it back toward Price Creek. When the creek becomes visible turn uphill, following a steep skid road and the creek. Switchback up to a small bench, then another, and then another. The creek disappears and the big disappointment appears—what looked like the ridge top from below turns out to be just another bench. Continue up, crossing Road (4834)124 to reach Road 4934 (4,320 feet).

If you followed Road (4834)124 up, simply ski across the snowmobile-groomed Road 4934 and continue up on Road (4934)126. This road is followed

Silver Peak viewed from Keechelus Ridge

to the radio towers. If you are going cross-country, continue straight up to the ridge crest. Contour to the right of a band of trees then head on up. The relay tower comes into view at the crest of the next ridge. The tower, reached at 4 miles (4,960 feet), is a good point to take in the view. Mount Rainier hovers above the southern forests while Mount Stuart dominates the eastern horizon. In between you will find Mount Margaret, Rampart Ridge, Box Ridge, Denny Mountain, Mount Catherine, Silver Peak, and more. Better pull out the map and learn all the bumps if you want to impress the next person you drag up here.

Round-trip skiers now make their way down the clearcuts and tree plantations, cutting turns back to the bottom. Non-telemark enthusiasts read on.

Loop Tour: From the summit relay towers, either head north along the ridge crest to find the groomed snowmobile route on the left (west) side of the ridge or ski back down Road (4934)126 to Road 4934. Go right and follow this road north. The road climbs gradually and the views are continuous. After following Road 4934 for 1¼ miles you will arrive at a major intersection with Road 4948 at 5¾ miles. Go straight. The road climbs for a short distance then begins a steady descent across the clearcut hillsides. At 7¼ miles pass the Mount Margaret Trailhead parking area on the left. Continue to descend, steeply now, for another ¼ mile then go left on Road (4832)135. This steep, but short, spur road soon reaches Road 4832 and ends. Go left and ski past Resort Creek Pond, then spend the next 2 miles in a steady descent to Resort Creek. The final 2 miles back to the Sno-Park are rolling, and tired muscles will have to do a bit of climbing as well as gliding before you finish the loop at 11½ miles.

8 RESORT CREEK POND

Class: *multiple use*
Rating: *more difficult*
Round trip: *8 miles*
Skiing time: *4 hours*
Elevation gain: *900 feet*

High point: *3,380 feet*
Best: *December–March*
Avalanche potential: *low*
Map: *Green Trails, Snoqualmie Pass No. 207*

Map on page 39

Skirting along the lower flanks of Keechelus Ridge is an excellent place for classical cross-country skiing and modern skating. It is also an ideal area for longer ski tours that use the extensive network of logging roads to explore the views from the ridge tops. The only disadvantage of this area is

View over Keechelus Lake and the surrounding hills

the number of snowmobiles you will find buzzing the roads and blitzing the clearcuts on weekends. If mingling with snowmobiles is not your idea of a good time, plan your trip here for midweek.

Access: Drive to the Westbound Price Creek Sno-Park as described in Tour 7 (2,560 feet).

The Tour: At the west end of the Sno-Park find the combined ski–snowmobile trail, which traverses a clearcut, crosses two creeks, then climbs steeply to intersect Forest Road 4832 at ½ mile. Go left on Road 4832 and head northwest on a groomed snowmobile trail that rolls through forest and clearcuts along the flanks of Keechelus Ridge. The grooming makes for easy skiing, and the miles will pass quickly as you cruise, glide, or skate past the occasional view of Keechelus Lake Dam and Meadow Creek valley.

At the 2-mile mark the road descends to cross Resort Creek (2,800 feet) then begins a steady climb; ignore several spur roads. The climb ends at a 3,380-foot saddle. Continue on another 50 feet to find Resort Creek Pond (3,300 feet) just off the road on the right at 4 miles. This sheltered little lake is an excellent spot for a picnic before heading back.

9 THAT DAM LOOP

Class: self-propelled
Rating: more difficult
Loop trip: 5 miles
Skiing time: 3 hours
Elevation gain: 80 feet

High point: 2,480 feet
Best: mid-December–February
Avalanche potential: low
Map: Green Trails, Snoqualmie Pass
No. 207

Map on page 44

Loops are fun and this one is no exception. Meander through the forest, cross a snow-laced stream, skim over the Yakima River, and ski across Keechelus Lake Dam on a trail perched at the very top.

Note: Since losing the very popular Crystal Springs/Stampede Pass Sno-Park area, the skier-only status of this Sno-Park is uncertain. Be prepared to share the first section of this loop with snowmobiles in the future.

Access: Drive Interstate 90 east 9.1 miles from Snoqualmie Pass summit to the Eastbound Price Creek Sno-Park (2,480 feet). (Westbound traffic must drive all the way to Hyak/Rocky Run Exit 54 to return to the Sno-Park.)

The Tour: The trail begins as an unsigned corridor through the trees that starts at the upper end of the parking lot. This road/trail heads west for 50 feet through the trees then turns abruptly left (south) at an unmarked intersection. Note the narrow road on the right; it is the return leg of the loop.

Wander through the forest on a quiet, nearly level skier trail. After a mile in the forest, the trail becomes a road and picnic tables announce arrival at Crystal Springs Campground. Shortly beyond is Stampede Pass Road No. 54. At the road you may need to remove your skis and walk. Go right, crossing the Yakima River on the car bridge. Continue along the road for 500 feet to an intersection with the road to the Crystal Springs/Stampede Pass Sno-Park (closed in 1994 but may reopen in the future). Stay to the left and continue to follow Road 54. Ski past the gate then up the broad road. Now brace yourself for the recreational equivalent of rush hour on Interstate 5. The road swarms with skiers, snowmobilers, Sno-Cats, and parades of people heading to private cabins. At 1¾ miles Forest Road 5480 branches off to the right. Stay to the left for another ¼ mile to the railroad grade where you will join the Iron Horse Trail. Go right and head up this peaceful corridor on groomed ski tracks.

After ½ mile of easy gliding the railroad grade passes under an avalanche shoot. When conditions are unstable it is best to descend to the road, ski past the hazard, then climb back to the railroad grade.

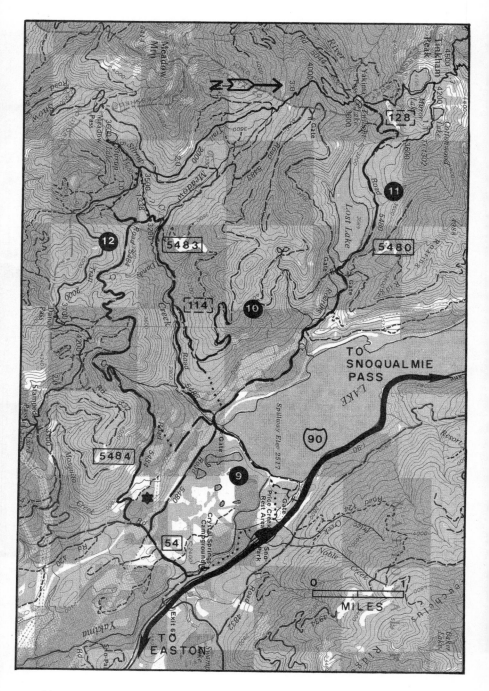

Small stream crossed on That Dam Loop

At the 4-mile point you will see Keechelus Lake Dam to your right. Make your third right turn here on the dam road. Cross over (or around) a snow-covered gate, then ski along the top of Keechelus Lake Dam. In good weather make this your picnic site, as it's the best viewpoint. Enjoy the snowcapped peaks rising above the lake and the ice-clogged Yakima River emerging from it.

On the far side of the dam, note the maintenance buildings in a clearing. Descend a ramp off the dam and ski across that clearing on the left side of the buildings, then head straight into the forest on a wide trail paralleling a line of telephone poles, which lead to an open flood plain. At this point you will find a trail, marked with blue diamonds, that heads off to the left. Follow it to a bridge and cross the stream.

Once across the stream, go right and climb a short, steep hill on an old, abandoned road. At the top take a left turn to return to the Sno-Park.

I-90 CORRIDOR

10 YAKIMA VALLEY OVERVIEW

Class: *multiple use*
Rating: *most difficult*
Round trip: *10 miles*
Skiing time: *5 hours*
Elevation gain: *1,420 feet*

High point: *3,900 feet*
Best: *mid-December–March*
Avalanche potential: *moderate*
Map: *Green Trails, Snoqualmie Pass No. 207*

Map on page 44

You would not want to visit the hills overlooking the Yakima River valley in the summer. The area has been so intensely logged that it's hard to find a tree to hide behind. Ironically, snows of winter mask the scars of summer and the hills appear virginally soft, beautiful, and white.

What is visible to the winter traveler, then, is a proliferation of viewpoints and overlooks. From the multitude of viewpoints, one particular area offers an outstanding overview of the Yakima River valley from the Snoqualmie Pass peaks down the length of Keechelus Lake, east over Amabilis Mountain, and all the way to the little town of Easton.

Access: Drive Interstate 90 east 9.1 miles from Snoqualmie Pass summit to the Eastbound Price Creek Sno-Park (2,480 feet). (Westbound traffic must drive all the way to Hyak/Rocky Run Exit 54 to return to the Sno-Park.)

The Tour: From the upper end of the Sno-Park, follow the unsigned ski trail into the forest for 50 feet. At an unmarked intersection, turn right onto

Keechelus Lake Dam and Yakima Valley from the Overview

a narrow, somewhat overgrown road heading down. Descend the short, steep hill to a swampy area and cross a small stream, then turn left and cross two channels of a larger stream on a solid bridge.

Once across the stream, climb a 10-foot bank to a level bench, then turn right and head north 1,000 feet to a wide trail. At this point you should ski to your left and follow the telephone lines to Keechelus Lake Dam. Using the ramp on the right side of the dam maintenance buildings, climb up to the crest of the dam then head to the left, skiing along the road on the top. Here you will witness fine views of the lake and surrounding peaks. Head left along the top of the dam for 1 mile to Road 5480.

Ski straight ahead on Road 5480, crossing the railroad tracks and the Meadow Creek Bridge, before reaching the Meadow Creek intersection. Here a choice of an approach by road or a combination of road and cross-country awaits you. The latter option is best left to skiers with *backcountry* experience.

The road approach follows Meadow Creek Road No. 5483, the left fork. The road heads up along the creek through a narrow canyon that widens into a broad valley. Near the edge of endless clearcuts (2,900 feet), at the 3-mile point of your tour, leave Road 5483 and go up and to your right on Road (5483)114, which leads you through a band of second-growth forest to open clearcuts. The objective of your tour, a flat platform, is reached at 5 miles (3,900). This platform is easy to find, distinguished by its location at the corner of a large switchback and by the excellent views.

The road climbs on, heading west over Meadow Creek valley, but if you've come for the views it doesn't get any better than this. Might as well sit down and enjoy a beer.

Cross-country Route: To the overview, pass the turnoff to Meadow Creek Road 5483 and continue right toward Lost Lake for about 500 feet, then go left on the next road (no road numbers posted). The road climbs steeply (climbing skins very helpful here) through a clearcut to the powerline road. Head left and follow the powerline road for about ⅛ mile. Now find a thin section in the band of trees above and bushwhack up to the next clearcut. Continue up to Road (5483)114, which you will intersect about 1 mile below the overview.

Anyone with a passable telemark or a good kick-turn will discover this tour has a lot more to offer than good views. You will get plenty of thrills following the cross-country route down through the clearcuts to the Lost Lake Road. Be sure to stay on the right of the clearcut slopes during the descent; the left side is steep and could slide.

I-90 CORRIDOR

11 ANOTHER LOST LAKE

Class: *multiple-use*
Rating: *most difficult*
Round trip: *10 miles*
Skiing time: *5 hours*
Elevation gain: *800 feet*

High point: *3,200 feet*
Best: *mid-December–February*
Avalanche potential: *moderate*
Map: *Green Trails, Snoqualmie Pass No. 207*

Map on page 44

We always wonder why this country has so many "Lost Lakes." Was it a misplaced early explorer, or was it a modern-day skier who got disoriented in the maze of logging roads crisscrossing these environs? Pay attention to the landmarks and you'll find this pretty lake in its cradle of high hills without much trouble. Fail to pay attention and you'll join those early explorers and recent cross-country skiers who wandered up the wrong valley.

Access: Drive Interstate 90 east 9.1 miles from Snoqualmie Pass summit to the Eastbound Price Creek Sno-Park (2,480 feet). (Westbound traffic must drive all the way to Hyak/Rocky Run Exit 54 to return to the Sno-Park.)

Keechelus Lake from Lost Lake Road

The Tour: Follow the route described in Tour 10, 1½ miles across Keechelus Lake Dam to the railroad tracks. Cross Meadow Creek to reach an intersection and go right on Road 5480, a groomed snowmobile raceway. The road remains nearly flat until it reaches a small community of resort homes at Roaring Creek near 3½ miles. Now the work begins as you start a steady ascent.

Arrive at a narrow pass at 4½ miles. On the far side is a view of 3,089-foot Lost Lake. The lake lies at the lower end of a broad valley amidst sweeping clearcuts. The only trees that remain standing here are a narrow fringe that encircles the lake. It's an odd sight to say the least. If staying the night, you will find nice camping along the northwest side of the lake.

If time allows after cheese and rolls, there is plenty of exploring to be done. Continue around the lake for another 1½ miles on Road 5480, then go left on Road (5480)128. Leave this road just above Yakima Pass and ski up a short, steep clearcut to a forested saddle where you will find 4,195-foot Mirror Lake nestled at the base of Tinkham Peak.

If your batteries are still charged, consider a loop trip. Ski toward Yakima Pass and descend 200 feet to little Twilight Lake, then head south to the ridge top and intersect one of several logging spur roads from Meadow Creek valley. Consult your map for various ways back to the Sno-Park.

12 THE DANDY LOOP

Class: *multiple use*
Rating: *most difficult*
Loop trip: *10½ miles*
Skiing time: *6 hours*
Elevation gain: *1,620 feet*

High point: *4,100 feet*
Best: *December–March*
Avalanche potential: *moderate*
Map: *Green Trails, Snoqualmie Pass No. 207*

Map on page 44

This tour has it all: flat country for striding, gliding, and skating; gentle upgrades for an aerobic workout; lunch spots complete with expansive views; and an exhilarating descent (with options for telemarkers). It's not called the Dandy Loop for nothing, you know.

The Dandy Loop is on multiple-use roads that are groomed for snowmobile use only. Although the grooming makes for easy skiing and occasionally for excellent skating, be prepared to encounter a lot of mechanical sleds on weekends. For a relatively peaceful tour—try midweek.

Access: Drive Interstate 90 east 9.1 miles from Snoqualmie Pass summit to the Eastbound Price Creek Sno-Park (2,480 feet). (Westbound traffic must drive all the way to Hyak/Rocky Run Exit 54 to return to the Sno-Park.)

The Tour: Follow the Tour 10 directions for the first 1½ miles. Cross the railroad grade and the Meadow Creek Bridge to reach an intersection. Turn left on Road 5483 and ski through a thin fringe of trees, then along the bald hillsides of Meadow Creek valley. At 4½ miles (3,160 feet), turn left onto Dandy Creek Road No. 5484. Recross Meadow Creek, then begin the long slog upward.

Pass the trail to Stirrup Lake at 4¾ miles. At 5 miles a spur road cuts off to the right, a tempting side trip to a small saddle. At 5¾ miles the road enters one of the rare groves of trees in this area where you can say a brief hello to a life form that is nearly extinct here. Ski across Dandy Creek (3,390 feet), then say goodbye to the trees because it's quickly back to the clearcuts.

At 6 miles the road skirts around a rugged basin at the lowest end of Dandy Pass. A final push brings its reward with a 4,100-foot high point, views over the entire Meadow Creek valley, Dandy Pass, and a dandy view of Mount Rainier. Peak baggers can conquer the clearcut hill just 100 feet above. The road skirts around the crest of the hill to begin its long descent back to the valley floor. The downward plunge begins with a sweeping semi-circle around a small pond. (If the snow is stable, consider a shortcut down and across the frozen pond to the road on the far side.)

Beyond the pond, follow the road and swoosh across a steep open hillside, past a band of trees, through a steep logging clearing, and then into a second clearing. This road does not receive regular grooming and the snowmobiles create a series of rollercoaster bumps that make the steep descent incredibly fascinating. When the road is icy, the descent creates an enlivening flow of adrenaline.

Road 5484 ends at Stampede Pass Road No. 54. Turn left and ski to the railroad grade. Go left and follow the groomed tracks of the Iron Horse Trail along the railroad grade. After ½ mile of easy striding, the railroad grade passes through an avalanche zone. If the snow is unstable, and it always is after any heavy snowfall or after a rainstorm, descend to the road and ski around the avalanche area. After ⅛ mile you can return to the railroad grade.

At 9 miles you will spot the dam access road on your right. Leave the railroad grade and follow your tracks back across the dam to reach the Sno-Park at 10½ miles.

Dandy Pass area; Tinkham Peak in distance

13 STAMPEDE PASS

Stampede Pass

Class: *multiple use*
Rating: *more difficult*
Round trip: *12 miles*
Skiing time: *6 hours*
Elevation gain: *1,300 feet*
High point: *3,700 feet*
Best: *December–March*
Avalanche potential: *low*
Map: *Green Trails, Snoqualmie Pass No. 207*

Loop Trip

Class: *multiple use*
Rating: *most difficult*
Loop trip: *12 miles*
Skiing time: *7 hours*
Elevation gain: *1,960 feet*
High point: *4,360 feet*
Best: *December–mid-March*
Avalanche potential: *moderate*
Map: *Green Trails, Snoqualmie Pass No. 207*

Miles of roads to climb, high-speed descents through open clearcuts, choice winter campsites, and delightful views all contribute to making Stampede Pass a most enjoyable day or weekend ski tour. Skiers of all ages and abilities could enjoy this trip but, due to a few snowmobilers who are still proving their manhood by rocketing, you need to be com-

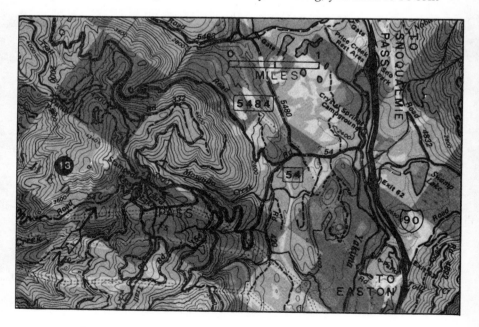

Skier on the Pacific Crest Trail, north of Stampede Pass

petent in your descending skills to truly enjoy this tour.

Many of the roads in the Stampede Pass area are regularly groomed for snowmobile use. The result is a track wide enough for skating. If you are skating, use special caution around snowmobiles; they may fail to account for the width of your stance. As always, the best way to avoid the snowmobiles is to plan a midweek tour.

Two tours are suggested here; a round-trip road tour to Stampede Pass and a loop tour that requires a moderate amount of cross-country navigation, a good map, and good weather so that you can find your landmarks.

Access: Drive Interstate 90 east 9.1 miles from Snoqualmie Pass summit to the Eastbound Price Creek Sno-Park (2,480 feet). (Westbound traffic must drive all the way to Hyak/Rocky Run Exit 54 to return to the Sno-Park.)

The Tour: Follow the directions given in Tour 9 for the first 2 miles to the Iron Horse Trail. Ski across the railroad tracks, and a few feet beyond pass a road on your right. This is the road you will descend if you choose to ski the entire loop. For now, stay with Road 54 as it swings left, starting the long climb to the pass.

Climb steadily to the powerline clearing at 3½ miles. At this point the road begins a short series of switchbacks where you will find excellent views of the Yakima River valley, Amabilis Mountain, and the Keechelus Ridge area. Near the 5-mile mark you will encounter another major intersection as Road 41 to Easton (popular with snowmobilers) branches left.

The slopes north of Stampede Pass

The Stampede Pass Road heads to the right and carves across the steep, forested walls of Mosquito Creek valley. As you climb, you will pass two roads on the right; the second one, Spur Road (5400)332, connects with Road 5484 and is groomed for snowmobiles. (This spur is the recommended route for skaters who wish to ski the entire loop.) At 6 miles the road crests the unpretentious summit of 3,700-foot Stampede Pass.

From Stampede Pass you can explore miles of connecting roads and open ridge tops. A favorite destination is Lizard Lake, a small, sheltered pond located just 300 feet beyond the pass on the left. Also consider a side trip to the U.S. government weather station located 1½ miles south (reached by a small road from Lizard Lake). Excellent campsites abound throughout this area.

If intending to ski the loop, the return trip is made by following the Pacific Crest Trail north. To find the trail, locate a narrow bench on the north side of the road about 300 feet on the east side of Stampede Pass. Ski along the narrow bench for about 100 feet, then go right and contour up to the base of a steep slope. (The trail is usually invisible at this point.) Stay in the trees on the left side of the ridge until you reach the ridge crest. Once on the ridge top follow the path of the Pacific Crest Trail. Using the ridge as a guide, ski along the west side of the crest and follow it over a second hill to a large clearcut valley.

Continue following the ridge as it meanders in a northwesterly direction to its end on a hilltop (4,360 feet) overlooking clearcut Meadow Creek valley. Turn left on the snowmobile-groomed Spur Road (5400)332, and ski the ridge down to a small saddle. Stay right and follow the road on a traverse across the side of a steep hill to a major, but unsigned, intersection. Take a sharp right on Road 5484 for a sweeping descent across a steep hillside. The road swings around a small lake and continues on a steady descent that lasts for 3 miles. The downhill rush ends at the Stampede Pass Road. Go left and ski across the old railroad grade at 10 miles. Follow Road 54 back to Crystal Springs Campground, then head back along the trail to reach the Sno-Park at 12 miles.

14 KACHESS CAMPGROUND

Class: *multiple use*
Rating: *easiest*
Round trip: *4 miles*
Skiing time: *2 hours*
Elevation loss: *20 feet*
High point: *2,320 feet*
Best: *January–February*
Avalanche potential: *none*
Maps: *Green Trails, Snoqualmie Pass No. 207 and Kachess Lake No. 208*

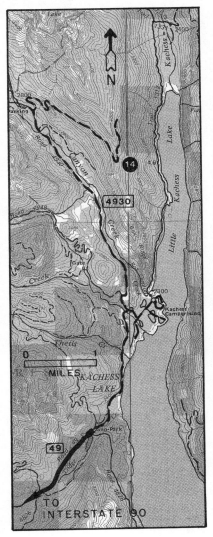

The tour to Kachess Campground is especially good for beginners, groups with varying abilities, or first-time winter campers. A gentle road swings around the lakeshore to forests of tall trees and a pleasant campground. Several miles of skiing in the campground and miles of road beyond it also tempt stronger skiers to work up a sweat.

This is a multiple-use area that is popular with snowmobilers. Midweek is the best time to find the quiet and solitude of winter.

Access: Follow Interstate 90 for 10.2 miles east of Snoqualmie Pass to Stampede Pass/Kachess Lake Exit 62. Drive east toward Kachess Lake for 3.3 miles to the long Sno-Park. Parking is only allowed on the south side of the road (2,320 feet). On busy weekends the area fills up fast, so try to arrive by 9:00 A.M.

The Tour: From the parking area a gentle descent leads to a broad view up and down Kachess Lake reservoir and across to the partially

Box Canyon Creek

shaved Kachess Ridge. After a brief stop to reorganize hats, mittens, and jacket zippers, and to check out the view, follow the road back into the forest.

After 1½ miles, cross Gale Creek, which marks the entrance to Kachess Campground. Several hours can be spent investigating this sprawling area. The campground loops make excellent racetracks, while nature loops offer challenging courses around the trees.

Skiers who would like to log a few more miles can stride along Forest Road 4930 for another 4 miles to the Rachel Lake Trailhead. Sweeping panoramas are in absence as you ski along Box Canyon Creek, but the steep-walled valley is very beautiful. Snow-plastered hillsides, towering evergreens with white coats, and ice sculptures along the banks of the creek all await you. Elevation gain for these extra miles is only 330 feet.

15 AMABILIS MOUNTAIN

Class: *self-propelled*
Rating: *most difficult*
Round trip: *8 miles*
Skiing time: *5 hours*
Elevation gain: *2,154 feet*

High point: *4,554 feet*
Best: *January–March*
Avalanche potential: *low*
Map: *Green Trails, Snoqualmie Pass No. 207*

Ski along the gleaming summit ridge of 4,554-foot Amabilis Mountain to views of Kachess and Keechelus Lakes, Stampede Pass, Mount Catherine, Silver Peak, and above all Mount Rainier. Telemarkers will find great slopes to carve their sweeping signatures on, while road tourers can count on an exciting cruise down on the logging road loop.

This very popular loop tour over the top of Amabilis Mountain is just one of several favorite activities that bring people to the Cabin Creek Sno-Park by the hundreds on most winter weekends. Tour 16, suitable for beginners, as well as racers using the very challenging groomed course for classical skiers and skaters (see And More Ski Tours), also uses this Sno-Park. Plan to arrive early, definitely before 10:00 A.M. to ensure a parking spot in

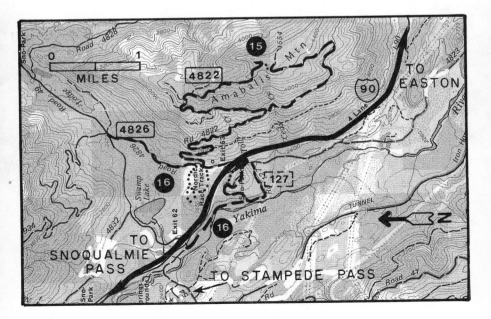

the lot. On race days this may not be early enough. If the Sno-Park is full, you will have to go elsewhere; cars that park in the interchange area will be ticketed and towed.

Access: Drive Interstate 90 east from Snoqualmie Pass 10.3 miles then take Cabin Creek Exit 63. The Sno-Park is located on the west side of the freeway (2,189 feet). If the upper lot is full, try the lower lot.

The Tour: From the Sno-Park, walk the overpass to the north side of the freeway and begin your tour on a broad snow-covered road. Ski past Trollhaugen Hut, operated by a cross-country racing club. The carefully groomed tracks are open to the public except on race days. Beyond the hut the road rounds a corner and splits. Go right on Amabilis Mountain Road and immediately start to climb.

The route switchbacks uphill, passing several old spur roads, first to the left, then to the right. Occasional windows in the forest give glimpses of massive Keechelus Ridge and the Swamp Lake area.

The first major intersection, reached at the 2-mile point (3,300 feet), marks the start of the loop portion of the tour. You can reach the top from either direction; however, for best enjoyment of the scenery go left. In the next mile

Keechelus Lake from Amabilis Mountain

the road will lead you across a massive clearcut to the north end of the mountain, then turn your skis back to the south with a sweeping switchback. At this point you are on open slopes, just below the crest of the long ridge that is Amabilis Mountain. From here on the road often is windswept and hard to follow (when visibility is poor, make the ridge top your turnaround). Ski to the crest of the ridge then follow it southwest. There is a road to follow, if you can find it, for most of the distance.

After 1¼ mile of scenic ridge-top skiing you will reach a line of trees. Go right and skirt along the west side of the trees for ¼ mile. You will first descend then traverse south to intersect a major road (4,470 feet).

For the loop return, go straight when you intersect the road and head down a long switchback to close the loop at 6 miles. This leg of the loop crosses a steep avalanche chute and should not be skied except in times of low avalanche hazard.

Telemarkers will find possibilities everywhere. Either head back the way you came and pick a likely looking slope or follow the loop route to more clearcuts on the southern end of the mountain.

I-90 CORRIDOR

16 CABIN CREEK

Cabin Creek Loop

Class: self-propelled
Rating: more difficult
Round trip: 1 mile
Skiing time: 1 hour
Elevation gain: 110 feet
High point: 2,560 feet
Best: January–February
Avalanche potential: none
Map: Green Trails, Snoqualmie
   Pass No. 207

Stampede Pass Road

Class: self-propelled
Rating: more difficult
Round trip: 3 miles
Skiing time: 2 hours
Elevation gain: none
High point: 2,450 feet
Best: January–February
Avalanche potential: none
Map: Green Trails, Snoqualmie
   Pass No. 207

Map on page 57

In the midst of mountain country where all the scenery is vertical, the Cabin Creek area features open and gentle terrain ideal for beginners to perfect their balance and racers to achieve speed. Two trips can be made. The first is a short, scenic loop trip that starts and ends at the parking lot. The second follows a narrow trail through the forest paralleling the Yakima River to the Stampede Pass Road.

Cabin Creek Loop

Access: Drive Interstate 90 east from Snoqualmie Pass 10.3 miles to Cabin Creek Exit 63. Park in the large Sno-Park on the west side (2,450 feet).

Cabin Creek Loop: The loop trip starts from the lower end of the Sno-Park and returns to the upper end.

From the base of the upper lot walk or ski down the dirt road to the lower lot. Stay to the left and follow the road past the lower lot following signs to the U-Fish and private campground. After 40 feet or so go right on a groomed road that swings around the lower end of the parking area then heads out through second-growth forest to open clearcuts. At all intersections go right, following the signs toward the viewpoint. (You might also enjoy a side-trip cruise out through the meadows to your left.) Your trail briefly swings close to the Yakima River then heads on around the hill. When the trail divides at ½ mile stay right and spend the next ¼ mile traversing a large clearcut. At ¾ mile the trail divides again. To exit the loop, go left and follow a narrow path back to the Sno-Park entrance. For views stay to the right and ski to the top of the hill where you may get a look at Amabilis Mountain to the east and Stampede Pass to the west.

Stampede Pass Road: From the lower parking area walk or ski down the dirt road that heads toward the U-Fish for 40 feet, then go right on a groomed ski trail. Ski through the second-growth forest to the clearcuts, then go right and head around the base of a knoll. When the Cabin Creek Loop and viewpoint trails branch off to the right, continue straight on a trail that soon heads back into the trees. The trail rolls over a few short hills, which makes for a couple of thrilling moments. You will also cross two small creeks while remaining in the forest throughout. At 1½ miles the trail ends at the Stampede Pass Road.

Note: The Stampede Pass Trail winds through heavy second-growth forest, crossing several small creeks. The tour is difficult when the snow cover is insufficient. This is not a good early- or late-season tour.

I-90 CORRIDOR

17 MORE CABIN CREEK

Class: *multiple use*
Rating: *easiest*
Round trip: *6 miles*
Skiing time: *2 hours or more*
Elevation loss: *200 feet in first 3 miles*

High point: *2,800 feet*
Best: *March–mid-May*
Avalanche potential: *low*
Maps: *Green Trails, Easton No. 240 and Lester No. 239*

Here's another one of those springtime trips that come into season once the noisy herd of snowmobiles has been put out to pasture. The Cle Elum Ranger District now ranks as Washington's number-one area for snowmobile use, so wintertime skiing anywhere in the district may remind you of running with the bulls in Pamplona. However, when the sun gets warm in the lowlands and the dandelions start sprouting in your garden, let the snowmobilers stay home to weed while you go skiing.

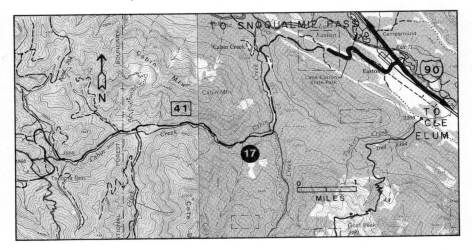

Log-reloading area on Cabin Creek Road

Diverse skiing opportunities await you here. Those who have yet to try out their Christmas skis (shame on you) can cruise the wide, rolling roads, long-distance skiers will find ample miles to exhaust themselves, and telemarkers will encounter steep, open clearcuts to carve.

Access: Drive Interstate 90 for 17 miles east of Snoqualmie Pass and take Exit 71 at Easton. Drive into town, cross the main street (old Highway 10), then head straight up Cabin Creek Road for 0.2 mile. After crossing the railroad tracks swing right, remaining on Cabin Creek Road. Drive to the snowline, usually about 1.5 miles from town in late March (2,800 feet).

The Tour: The road is groomed for snowmobiles throughout the winter, so expect a solid (i.e., icy) surface in the early morning. Ski along rolling terrain, past a swamp, and through tall timber for nearly 1½ miles before descending to the first viewpoint over the Yakima River to the clearcut slopes of Amabilis Mountain. The road continues dropping to an intersection at 2½ miles. Here, take the left fork (Forest Road 41) and ski to the large log reloading area, which when snow-covered looks like an open meadow. This is a good place for first-time skiers to snack before heading back.

Skiers out for a workout or weekend can continue on up Road 41, which joins a network of roads around Cabin Mountain. It's 7 more miles to Tacoma Pass (3,400 feet), 15 miles to Stampede Pass, and 30 miles to Snoqualmie Pass. If endless miles of roads fail to motivate you, will a good viewpoint rev your engine? If so, ski 3 more miles up Cabin Creek to a viewpoint overlooking the entire Keechelus Lake area.

18 HEX MOUNTAIN

Class: *multiple use*
Rating: *backcountry*
Round trip: *8 miles*
Skiing time: *6 hours*
Elevation gain: *2,647 feet*

High point: *5,034 feet*
Best: *December–April*
Avalanche potential: *low*
Map: *Green Trails, Kachess Lake No. 208*

You might call Hex Mountain an "exceptional" backcountry tour. Routefinding is exceptionally confusing on the logging-road portion of the tour and exceptionally easy on the backcountry portion. The tour is exceptionally free from avalanche hazard, making it skiable in all conditions. The descent through open forest and meadows provides exceptional fun. Finally, you will find some exceptional views at the tour's high point at the summit.

There are two approaches to Hex Mountain. The approach described here

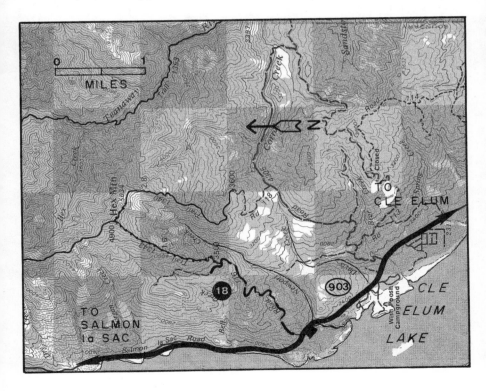

Cle Elum Lake from Hex Mountain

is the shorter and steeper of the two. The longer approach (from Road 4305 and Trail 1340) is exceptionally overrun by snowmobiles on weekends. (Rumor says it is a good midweek tour.)

Access: Drive Interstate 90 to Exit 80. Go east to State Route 903, then take a left and head north 8.7 miles, passing through Roslyn, Ronald, and Lakedale. Park in a small turnout on the left side of the road at Newport Creek (2,387 feet).

The Tour: From the turnout, walk north on the road for 0.1 mile to Forest Road (4300)116 (the first road on the right). Don the skis here and start the climb. The forest around Road (4300)116 has been selectively cut, and roads and skid roads branch off in all directions. As a result, our explanation may seem incomplete and routefinding will be a challenge for the first 1½ miles of the tour. Be sure to avoid the new road located ¾ mile up, which heads on a long ascending traverse to the right.

The road climbs steeply for the first mile then levels out to contour around a small catch basin. Study your map and ignore all side roads as you skirt around the left side of the basin. The road drops, climbs briefly, levels out for a second time, then divides. Take the left fork, traversing uphill. (If the road starts descending steadily, you took the wrong fork.)

Your goal is the summit of the ridge to your left. To reach the ridge the road climbs across the hillside, dips left into a small side valley, then climbs again. Around 3,200 feet, the road divides again—stay left.

At 2 miles (3,500 feet), the road reaches the ridge top. Leave the road here and ski to the right, heading up the crest of the ridge. Under the snow is Trail 1343, and you may see signs of it, such as blazes on trees and clear passages through the forest.

The ridge climbs (with occasional dips) for the next 1¾ miles. Stay away from the edges, which are often corniced. At 4,900 feet, the ridge you have followed reaches the summit ridge and ends. Go right (southeast) for the final ¼ mile, first descending, then climbing out of the trees to the open summit of 5,034-foot Hex Mountain.

Atop you will find a lot of scenery to soak in while eating lunch. To the west lie Cle Elum Lake and a host of minor summits between Mount Baldy and Thorp Mountain. To the north rise the rugged summits of Cone Mountain and Davis Peak as well as the rounded slopes of Sasse Mountain. Finally, Table Mountain and the open plains of the Yakima River valley occupy the eastern view.

CLE ELUM LAKE

19 FRENCH CABIN CREEK

Class: *multiple use*
Rating: *most difficult*
Round trip: *4–14 miles*
Skiing time: *4 hours–2 days*
Elevation gain: *1,336 feet*

High point: *3,600 feet*
Best: *March–mid-May*
Avalanche potential: *low–moderate*
Map: *Green Trails, Kachess Lake No. 208*

Map on page 66

A logging road with a number of short spurs leads to a variety of destinations and views, suitable for a good half-day workout, an all-day exploration, or an overnight up the Thorp Creek Trail. The trip is very good all winter—assuming the county road can be driven to Salmon la Sac. (In midwinter it is wise to call the Cle Elum Ranger Station to check on this.) Thanks to the Forest Service, however, the French Cabin Creek Road is heavily used on weekends by speeding snowmobiles; therefore, it is best for skiers to come midweek or wait until late spring when the snowmobiles give up.

Access: Take Exit 80 off Interstate 90 and drive to Highway 903. Go left, following signs to Salmon la Sac, passing through both Roslyn and Ronald and around Cle Elum Lake. At 12 miles from Roslyn City Hall, find French Cabin Creek Road No. 4308 on your left (2,262 feet).

The Basic Tour: The French Cabin Creek Road crosses the Cle Elum River on a concrete bridge and in ¼ mile starts climbing. In the next 2 miles the road gains 1,000 feet in a series of five long switchbacks, steep enough for most skiers. To escape snowmobile ruts, the first four switchbacks can be shortcut. As the road climbs, the face of Red Mountain comes in view, seemingly towering overhead, a spectacular sight after a fresh snowfall. At 2½ miles the road levels and enters French Cabin Creek valley. Reach the first major intersection at 3½ miles with the Thorp Creek Road.

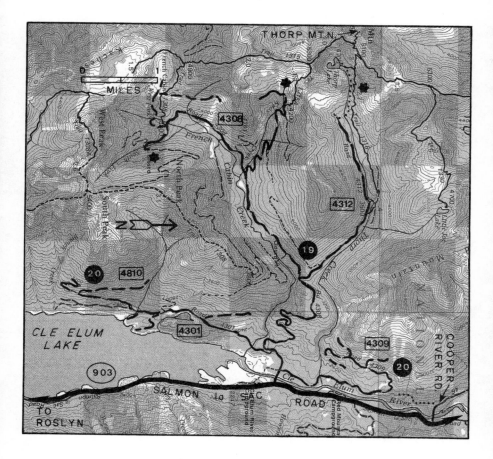

Thorp Creek Trail: Energetic *backcountry* skiers can do an overnight ski tour to Thorp Lake. After skiing up the French Cabin Creek Road for 3½ miles, go right on Thorp Creek Road No. 4312 for about 2½ miles to its end. Next head cross-country. Ski through the trees, climbing steadily to the right. If possible, cross to the north side of Thorp Creek. Follow the creekbed for the final mile to Thorp Lake. The forest travel is not easy—but it does stop the machines.

Camp at the lake in forest well away from any possible avalanche (but not under a tree topped with a mushroom of snow). Do not attempt the open slopes to the ridge above unless the snow is stable.

North Peak Road: From the Thorp Creek Road intersection at 3½ miles stay left and on French Cabin Creek Road No. 4308. Continue on for ½ mile then take a left (no road number was visible in 1994). Ski to a T intersection and go left. At the second intersection, take the right fork. The logging road climbs to clearcuts on North Peak; views of Red Mountain and up the Salmon la Sac Valley are great.

Knox Creek: From the intersection with the Thorp Creek Road at

Skiing the French Cabin Creek valley below Red Mountain

3½ miles, follow the left fork, Road 4308, for another 1½ miles. At 5 miles from the start go right on the Knox Creek Road and climb 2 miles to the end at the foot of a large, steep mountain meadow. (Avalanche hazard is possible in the meadow.)

French Cabin Mountain: From the intersection at 3½ miles, continue up Road 4308 for another 3½ miles to clearcuts and mountain meadows under French Cabin Mountain. At 7 miles the road divides. The left fork climbs to a point just short of the 5,461-foot summit of North Peak. The right fork meanders through French Creek Basin.

20 CLE ELUM RIVER

Class: *multiple use*
Rating: *easiest*
Round trip: *2–5 miles*
Skiing time: *1–2 hours*
Elevation gain: *none*

High point: *2,400 feet*
Best: *January–February*
Avalanche potential: *none*
Map: *Green Trails, Kachess Lake No. 208*

Map on page 66

A delightful valley-bottom tour within constant sight and sound of the Cle Elum River and with a fair chance of getting away from sight and sound of snowmobiles.

This tour comes in three easy parts; enjoy the scenery and the crisp winter air.

Access: The tour has two trailheads. You can ski from either the French Cabin Creek Road (see Tour 19 for driving directions) or Cooper River Road (see Tour 23 for driving directions). Unfortunately, steep cliffs and the crossing of Thorp Creek make it impossible to start at one point and finish at the other.

Davis Peak from the Cle Elum River

French Cabin Creek: This trailhead offers two destinations and 13½ miles of skiing. From the parking area (2,262 feet), follow the French Cabin Creek Road across the Cle Elum River bridge then take the first right on Road 4309. Ski north, paralleling the river for 1½ miles, until the road makes a switchback and starts to climb. If you choose to continue, the road will gain 500 feet in the next 1½ miles before ending in clearcuts. If the snowmobile brigades are out patrolling in force and the snow cover is sufficient, abandon the roads as soon as you are across the bridge and ski along the river. If snowmobiles are buzzing around and ruining your ski tracks, weave between the trees.

The alternative route begins ¼ mile past the Road 4309 turnoff. Find Road 4301 on the left and follow it for 2 miles to an intersection that makes a good turnaround point. However, if your skis are not ready to go back into storage, go right on Road 4810. Ski past the gate and climb for 1½ miles to clearcuts and views.

Cooper River Road: From Cooper River Road cross the Cle Elum River on a concrete bridge and as soon as practical leave the road on the downstream (left) side and follow as close to the river as you can. In roughly 1 mile cliffs and creeks stop progress.

CLE ELUM LAKE

21 JOLLY AND JOLLY TOO

Jolly Road

Class: multiple use
Rating: easiest
Round trip: 4 miles
Skiing time: 3 hours
Elevation gain: 1,720 feet
High point: 4,000 feet
Best: January–mid-April
Avalanche potential: low
Map: Green Trails, Kachess Lake
No. 208

Jolly Too Road

Class: multiple use
Rating: more difficult
Round trip: 8 miles
Skiing time: 4 hours
Elevation gain: up to 3,040 feet
High point: 5,400 feet
Best: January–mid-April
Avalanche potential: low
Map: Green Trails, Kachess Lake
No. 208

Map on page 70

Two fun logging roads on the east side of the Cle Elum River climb to open slopes and views, views, views. From grand overlooks you'll look down on the Cle Elum River Valley and over to French Cabin Creek, Red Mountain, and the Dutch Miller Gap Peaks. From Jolly Too your grand vista

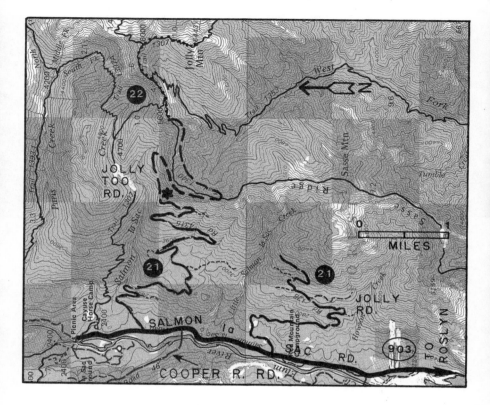

will extend north to Davis Peak and Mount Daniel. Best of all, both of these roads are considered too short to be of any great interest to snowmobilers. And although there is no official designation to ensure the tranquility of your tour, you rarely will see the mass packs of screaming motor sleds that invade the other roads in the Cle Elum River drainage.

Access: West of the town of Cle Elum, take Exit 80 off Interstate 90 then follow Highway 903 through the towns of Roslyn and Ronald and go around Cle Elum Lake. At 13.6 miles from Roslyn City Hall, park in a very small, plowed turnout on the right side of the road (2,300 feet). There are no signs, but this is the start of Jolly Road No. (4300)128.

Jolly Too Road No. 4315 is located another 1.6 miles up-valley. There is a small turnout and parking area on the right (2,360 feet). If no parking space is available, return 0.4 mile to Cooper River Road and walk back. (*Note:* A snowmobile Sno-Park is planned for this area, which will change the parking situation for the better but possibly ruin the skiing.)

A jolly view from a jolly clearcut

Jolly Road: After 1 mile of gentle climbing the road reaches a large bench (2,500 feet). The several-acre expanse of low, rolling bumps and flat bowls is ideal for family play. For views continue up the road another mile to the base of a large clearcut. In stable snow conditions, ascend approximately 700 feet to the top of the clearcut, for the sheer joy of carving a set of turns or sitzmarks on the way back down.

Jolly Too Road: Jolly Too Road is very similar to Jolly Road except a little steeper. Be sure to ski at least 2½ miles to a superb viewpoint north and west. At 2¾ miles the road swings around a level marsh; stay left, then begin a switchbacking ascent up the steep hillside. Pass a weather station to reach the turnaround point on a sharp corner at 4 miles (4,500 feet). At this point you are surrounded by massive clearcuts and incredible views.

The road continues, making a level traverse over an incredibly steep, wind-blown, and avalanche-prone hillside. Do not continue; instead, settle down to enjoy the view and a good lunch before rocketing back down the road to your car.

22 JOLLY MOUNTAIN

Winter's best decorations

Class: *multiple use*
Rating: *backcountry*
Round trip: *15 miles*
Skiing time: *8 hours*
Elevation gain: *4,083 feet*
High point: *6,443 feet*
Best: *December–April*
Avalanche potential: *moderate*
Map: *Green Trails, Kachess Lake
No. 208*

Map on page 70

Jolly Mountain provides an excellent introduction to backcountry skiing with a summit and impressive views as rewards for a lot of hard work. Easy navigation, lack of hazards (except near the summit), few technical difficulties, and premier picnic spots also combine to make this tour a popular one.

Access: Take Exit 80 off Interstate 90 and drive Highway 903 through the towns of Roslyn and Ronald then around Cle Elum Lake. At 15.2 miles from Roslyn City Hall (or 0.4 mile past Cooper River Road), watch for Forest Road 4315 on the right. Park off the road in the small two-car space (2,360 feet). (*Note:* A snowmobile Sno-Park is planned for this trail. If completed, the parking situation will improve.)

The Tour: For the first 4 miles, ski up Road 4315 through massive clearcuts, following the directions for Jolly Too Road given in Tour 21. Better yet, after the first 2 miles put on climbing skins and make a beeline toward the top of the ridge.

A sharp corner at the 4-mile point (4,500 feet) marks the spot where you will leave the road and head up a very steep and somewhat exposed clearcut to the ridge crest. (The road continues on, not only crossing a dangerous slope just beyond the corner, but also adding an extra 1½ miles to the summit.) Use caution as you climb this steep, clearcut hillside, staying near trees or the ridge crest, and avoid the gullies and open slopes that could slide.

You will reach the top of Sasse Ridge at around the 4,920-foot point. Here you will rejoin the road for a gradual climb along the south side of the ridge. When the road divides, stay right, skiing under a forested knoll to reach the end of the road and a corniced trailhead parking area at 5 miles (5,400 feet).

To continue, head east staying just to the right of the ridge crest. Jolly Mountain comes into view across the valley, as do the profiles of Davis Peak, Cone Mountain, and Red Mountain. After 6½ miles, the ridge rounds the end of a basin and reaches a 6,100-foot high point. Follow the ridge south, descending across a saddle to Jolly Mountain.

For the final ascent, follow the north ridge, staying as close to the crest as possible. Steep slopes here create some avalanche hazard in unstable conditions. The 6,443-foot summit of Jolly Mountain is reached at 7½ miles. Make a cautious 360-degree turn on the narrow rib looking south to Mount Rainier, down to Cle Elum Lake, west to the Dutch Miller Gap Peaks, north to Mount Daniel, and east to Mount Stuart. West and just below the summit is a broad open bench perfectly situated for gathering your MTRs (maximum tanning rays) and devouring a well-earned lunch.

Skier approaching the summit of Jolly Mountain

23 PETE LAKE AND COOPER PASS

Class: multiple use
Rating: more difficult
Round trip: 5–22 miles
Skiing time: 3 hours–overnight
Elevation gain: 1,000 feet

High point: 3,400 feet
Best: late spring but good all winter
Avalanche potential: low–moderate
Map: Green Trails, Kachess Lake No. 208

The Cooper River Road offers four different destinations, all with spectacular views of the Dutch Miller Gap Peaks—Lemah Mountain, Chimney Rock, Overcoat Peak, Summit Chief, and Bears Breast Mountain.

Access: Drive from Roslyn toward Salmon la Sac (see Tour 22 for directions) and at 14.8 miles from Roslyn City Hall find Cooper River Road (2,400 feet) on the left. During the winter months your tour will start here; however, as the snow melts in the spring, you can head up the road to find the more spectacular destinations listed below.

The Tour: During the shortest days of winter, your tour will begin with a long cruise up the Cooper Creek Road. The road receives regular grooming for the snowmobiles that cruise its length in long, noisy packs. The skiing is easy on this well-packed road that gains only 300 feet in the first 4¾ miles to the major junction and the four alternatives. If skiing in the mid- or late spring, you should be able to drive to this point.

Cooper Pass: From the major junction go straight ahead, climbing clearcuts with fine views of Cooper Lake and the Dutch Miller Gap Peaks. At 3 miles from the junction reach 3,400-foot Cooper Pass. For better views go higher on one of the many logging roads that climb up to your left on No Name Ridge. Cooper Pass is a great destination; unfortunately, it's great for snowmobiles also.

Cooper Lake: Go right, downhill, ¼ mile and cross the Cooper River on a concrete bridge. Follow the road as it curves left another ¼ mile, and find a spur that drops to Owhi Campground and the lakeshore (2,788 feet), ¾ miles from the major junction.

Tired Creek: Cross the Cooper River (see Cooper Lake, above), keep right at the campground–lakeshore junction, and follow Road 4616 past Tired Creek to its very end at 3,400 feet, 3¾ miles from the major junction.

This trip has excellent views of the Dutch Miller Gap Peaks but crosses two avalanche gullies, so do not try it for a couple of weeks after a heavy

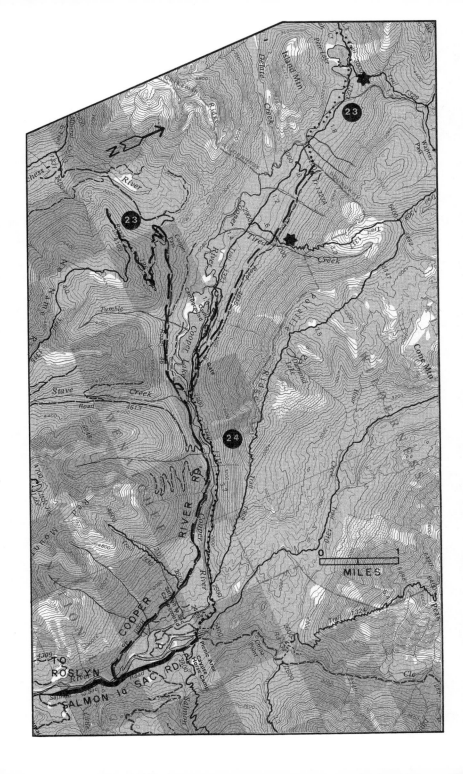

snowstorm or if the weather is unseasonably warm. If the avalanches have been massive enough, they will block the snowmobiles.

Pete Lake: This is the only place in the watershed where one can get away from machines and is recommended as an overnight trip for skiers with *backcountry* skills and equipment during the winter months only. From the road-end beyond Tired Creek, traverse downward in a clearcut, then in forest, to the valley bottom and go upstream 2½ miles to Pete Lake and a great view of mountains (11 miles from the Salmon la Sac Road). The way through the forest is not easy when the snow is deep and there are "wells" around trees, or when it's not deep enough to bridge the half-dozen tributary streams. The route is subject to large avalanches, including an area just short of the lake.

Skier on Road 4616 near Tired Creek; Lemah Mountain and Chimney Rock in distance

24 COOPER RIVER TRAIL

Class: *self-propelled*
Rating: *backcountry*
Round trip: *8 miles*
Skiing time: *5 hours*
Elevation gain: *400 feet*

High point: *2,900 feet*
Best: *January–February*
Avalanche potential: *low*
Map: *Green Trails, Kachess Lake*
  No. 208

Map on page 75

Want to sneak away from the annoying whirl and whiz of pesky snow-mobiles? The Cooper River Trail, wandering through the serene forests of the Salmon la Sac area, provides just such luxury. During the summer, two people can easily walk abreast along this broad trail, but winter snows transform this easy stroll into a challenging obstacle course. The trail narrows down to a thin thread, and skis must be negotiated around tight switchbacks, between trees, and over deep tree wells, with a lot of ups and downs. Better have good control of those boards if you don't intend to repeat Humpty Dumpty's great fall.

Access: Drive Interstate 90 to Roslyn–Salmon la Sac Exit No. 80 and go northeast for 3 miles. Turn left on State Highway 903 and drive 17 miles to the Salmon la Sac Guard Station. The driveable road usually ends here.

The Tour: Ski past the guard station, then just before the main road to Fish Lake begins climbing go left toward the campground. Ski across the Cle Elum River and turn right at the campground entrance gate. A few hundred feet farther a large Forest Service sign indicates the start of Cooper River Trail No. 1311 and Waptus River Trail No. 1310. With the Cooper River Trail all but invisible under the blanket of snow, follow a northwest bearing across the

Cooper River Trail

77

broad flats near the trailhead, heading away from the summer homes along the Cle Elum River. As the terrain begins to rise, ski left along the base of a hill until reaching the Cooper River. If you are on the trail, you will find summer homes on the left and forest on the right.

If the trail is not obvious, don't worry. Pick a route a couple hundred feet away from the river and ski up the valley. By late February the trail becomes evident, but do not feel constrained to follow it. If the trail gets too close to the river, move uphill. If the trail makes a difficult creek crossing, find a better one.

After ¾ mile the Polallie Ridge Trail branches off. The Cooper River is now in a deep canyon and at 1½ miles the trail reaches its 2,900-foot high point. The trail ends at Forest Road 4616 near Cooper Lake at 3½ miles. Turn right and follow snowmobile tracks for ½ mile to Owhi Campground with its lakeshore views. If you're still feeling spunky and want to log extra miles, see Tour 23.

25 WENATCHEE MOUNTAINS

Class: *multiple use*
Rating: *more difficult*
Round trip: *2 miles or more*
Skiing time: *3 hours–all day*
Elevation gain: *up to 2,500 feet*

High point: *5,700 feet*
Best: *mid-December–March*
Avalanche potential: *low*
Map: *Green Trails, Thorp No. 242*

If you are a gambler at heart, the ski terrain at the southwest end of the Wenatchee Mountains will captivate you. "What's the big gamble?" you ask. "Snow," is the answer. Some days you will encounter massive amounts of unconsolidated snow blanketing the slopes. A few days later, entire hillsides are once again naked.

Hit the snow right and the experience will include the exhilaration of skiing over open hillsides and rolling ridge tops with panoramic views. You will also find miles of roads and trails to explore, allowing for excellent day and overnight trips. Hit it wrong and rocks will carve glacial valleys into the bases of your skis. Obviously, if you are not a gambler, a few phone calls can help you decide whether to make the pilgrimage to this unpredictable neck of the woods.

Access: Drive Interstate 90 to Ellensburg and take Exit 106, then turn north. Immediately off the overpass is a four-way intersection with gas stations, fast-food joints, and few road signs. Turn left (west) following the

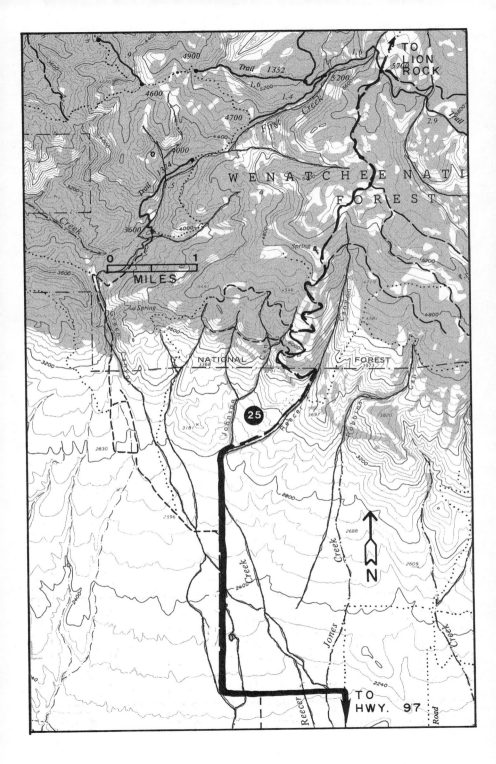

TO
LION
ROCK

Trail 1352
1.6
5200
1.4

5700

5200

2.9
Trail

Creek

4900

4600

4700

4400

4000

Trail 1314

.5

3600

4000

WENATCHEE NATL

FOREST

Creek

Spring

0   1

MILES

3600

Spring

3600

4546

4719

4800

4581

NATIONAL

FOREST

3368

3973

3951

25

3697

3820

3181

Johnson

Reecer

Cobb

3200

2830

2800

2596

2688

2609

N

2400

Creek

Jones

Creek

Creek

2240

TO
HWY.   97

Reecer

Road

Creek

Ski trail markers on the crest of Table Mountain

Highway 97 signs on an unmarked road, and drive 1.3 miles to another four-way intersection. Go left on the combined Highway 10 and 97, following it north 1.2 miles before taking a right on Highway 97. Follow Highway 97 for 1 mile, then take a right on Lower Green Canyon Road and drive north 5 miles to its end. Turn left on the Reecer Creek Road for 2.8 miles to the Sno-Park located at the end of the county road.

The Sno-Park here is a two-parter. The first part is located at the end of the county road (2,700 feet), but when snow cover is insufficient the road is open for another 2 miles to a small parking area at 3,200 feet.

The Tour: The open slopes around the Sno-Park are privately owned, so follow the road up the first looping switchback to the top of a bench, where it is possible to leave the road and ski up the open hill using the ridge line as a guide. The road continues to switchback, and skiers climbing the ridge can expect to cross it several times.

Views out over Ellensburg's vast plains, the Cascades, Mount Adams, and Mount Rainier are outstanding. The pine forests of the east side are also outstanding. Trees are small and thinly spread, allowing for cross-country skiing in the true sense of the word—a refreshing change for west-siders. Reecer Canyon, falling away on the right, is a gash in the open hillside, with striking cliffs of columnar basalt.

At 4 miles (4,800 feet) the switchbacks end at a group of summer homes. Return to the road here as it continues to climb, reaching a broad intersection at 5 miles (5,700 feet). You have now reached the southern end of Table

Mountain. You will find excellent touring here and limitless campsites in all directions—help yourself.

If time permits, ski north 6 miles to Lion Rock and an outstanding view over the Yakima River valley and Taneum Ridge area. If time is limited check out the "Skier Only" trails. Start from the intersection and go straight following the blue diamonds; the first is located right above the road sign. Ski into the trees following the blue diamonds to a clearing, where the Ellensburg Cross-Country Ski Club has a small warming hut. Several other trails start from the hut.

---

26 TEANAWAY RIVER AND BEAN CREEK BASIN

Teanaway River

Class: multiple use
Rating: easiest
Round trip: 4 miles or more
Skiing time: 2 hours or more
Elevation gain: 240 feet
High point: 2,500 feet
Best: January–February
Avalanche potential: low
Map: Green Trails, Mount Stuart No. 209

Bean Creek Basin

Class: multiple use
Rating: backcountry
Round trip: 6 miles
Skiing time: 5 hours
Elevation gain: 2,900 feet
High point: 6,500 feet
Best: April
Avalanche potential: high
Map: Green Trails, Mount Stuart No. 209

Maps on page 82

Yes, the Teanaway River Road sees a lot of snowmobile traffic. Yes, the area has acquired a bad reputation among skiers. So do we recommend skiing here? Yes, yes, yes!

Despite the inconvenience of skiing among a gaggle of machines, midwinter skiing on the beautiful road bordering the Teanaway River can be a joy. You'll be treated to large scenic meadows, gently rolling terrain, and exhilarating views of the Stuart Range. And once the snow melts in the river valley, it's time to put on the climbing skins and head up to the Bean Creek Basin high country for its outstanding telemark runs and panoramic views.

Access: Exit Interstate 90 just south of Cle Elum and follow Highway 970 for 5 miles. Turn north (left) on the Teanaway River Road. When the road divides, stay with the North Fork. At 9 miles from Highway 970 the plowing ends; park here (2,320 feet), or continue onward to the snowline, wherever that is.

Because this is a low-elevation trip, the snowline fluctuates wildly—especially in December. If you drive beyond the end of the plowed road, be sure and get out fast if snow starts falling. No plows will come to rescue you and your vehicle beyond the Lick Creek turnoff.

Teanaway River: From the snowplow turnaround, ski up the road paralleling the North Fork Teanaway River. After 1½ miles the road crosses the river and heads through the first of a series of meadows. At 2 miles Mount

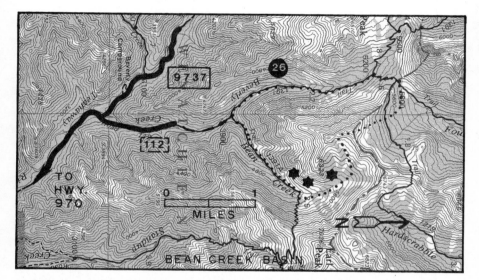

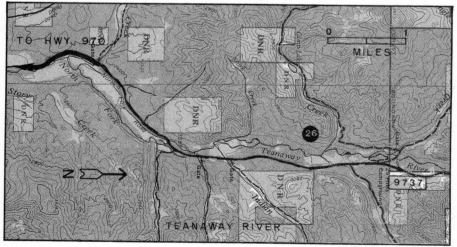

Stuart and its satellites suddenly come into view. Take a good look, then continue on through the trees and more views in the next ¾ mile.

At 4¼ miles the road passes 29 Pines Campground then divides (2,560 feet). This makes a good turnaround point or overnight campsite. If you drove this far without encountering snow, take the right fork and continue up the valley toward Esmerelda Basin, where the skiing should be good.

Bean Creek Basin: To reach the excellent springtime backcountry skiing of Bean Creek Basin, drive the Teanaway River Road then the North Fork Teanaway River Road 13.2 miles to 29 Pines Campground. Go right for 3.9 miles on Road 9737 to the Beverly Creek Bridge. Just before crossing the

Crossing Bean Creek

creek, turn uphill on Road (9737)112 and drive 1.1 miles to the end of the road (3,600 feet).

Start on the Beverly Turnpike Trail (an abandoned logging road), climbing through a clearcut for ¼ mile before reaching the actual trail. The trail climbs up the valley for 20 feet then divides at Bean Creek. Turn right just before the creek and head uphill on the Bean Creek Trail.

Parallel Bean Creek, climbing steeply up a narrow valley for ¼ mile, before making a careful crossing over the creek. Continue up-valley using the trees for shelter from possible avalanches or sloughs whenever possible. Cross over two avalanche gullies before the valley bends sharply north entering lower Bean Creek Basin, 1½ miles from the car.

Here the valley opens up into wide meadows. Watch for avalanches from the rock walls above, especially after snowfall or during warm weather. Stay off the inviting slopes and ski up the valley bottom, paralleling Bean Creek. Follow the valley and creek as they bend west, then make a short and steep ascent to the upper basin. Continue west to the upper bowls and climb toward the summits at the valley head. Watch for cornices toward the ridge tops (6,500 feet).

If you're game for more adventure and have a good map in tow, ski out of Bean Creek Basin into the Fourth Creek basin, over a 5,600-foot saddle, and return to the car via the Beverly Turnpike Trail.

---

27 RED TOP MOUNTAIN LOOKOVER

Camp robber searching for crumbs in the snow

Class: *multiple use*
Rating: *most difficult*
Round trip: *17 miles*
Skiing time: *8 hours–2 days*
Elevation gain: *2,560 feet*
High point: *5,280 feet*
Best: *January–April*
Avalanche potential: *low*
Maps: *Green Trails, Liberty No. 210 and Mount Stuart No. 209*

A giant panoramic view of Mount Stuart, Table Mountain, Mount Ingalls, Mount Rainier, Mount Adams, Swauk River valley, and the Teanaway River valley is

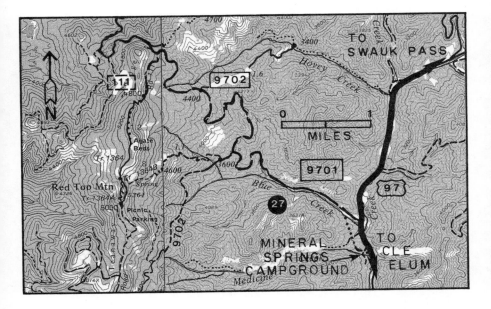

the object of this tour to the crest of Teanaway Ridge. Less than ½ mile away, perched high atop a rocky fortress, is Red Top Lookout, defended against skiers by snow- and ice-covered rock.

The trip is long, requiring a full day or overnight. The first 6 miles are on well-graded logging roads made noisy and icy by snow-blitzers. The last 2½ miles are up an old skid road, then a trailless hillside, to a forested ridge top, very difficult to climb when icy.

Access: Drive Highway 97 to Mineral Springs Resort (a small restaurant) then turn left to find the Sno-Park in Mineral Springs Campground on the west side of the road (2,720 feet). (When the snow has inched up the hillside, continue up Highway 970 for 0.1 mile, then go left on Road 9701 and drive to the snowline.)

The Tour: From the Sno-Park ski up a short, steep hill to a skid road. Go right and follow this road to Road 9701. Once you reach Road 9701, turn the tips of your skis to the west (left) and begin the long grind up the Blue Creek drainage. After the first mile, Red Top Mountain Lookout makes an occasional appearance through the trees.

Road 9701 meets Road 9702 at 3 miles and ends. To the left is Red Top Mountain Lookout; however, you need to stay right. At 6 miles, near the top of the ridge, find an ill-defined skid road, No. (9702)111, on your left (4,810 feet). Follow this narrow road as it contours along the ridge to the road-end in a small, steep clearcut at the 7-mile point. Now climb to the ridge top.

Red Top Lookout from "The Battlefield"

Once on the crest continue south ½ mile through trees to the broad, open area of "The Battlefield," well known by the rockhounds who in summer dig pits and trenches, searching for agates. The winter restores peace, permitting skiers to serenely enjoy the views.

28 IRON CREEK

Class: *self-propelled*
Rating: *easiest*
Round trip: *6 miles*
Skiing time: *3 hours*
Elevation gain: *700 feet*

High point: *3,600 feet*
Best: *mid-December–mid-March*
Avalanche potential: *low*
Map: *Green Trails, Liberty No. 210*

Map on page 88

Ironically, in an area where snowmobiles are the dominant life form, the Iron Creek Road provides sanctuary from the iron herd. This road is closed to snowmobilers and, as a result, the narrow little valley offers families and beginning skiers a quiet haven.

Access: Drive 8.8 miles north along Highway 97 from the intersection of Highways 97 and 970 (or 7.8 miles west from Swauk Pass) to Iron Creek Road No. 9714. Park at a small pull-out on the north side of the highway (2,900 feet).

The Tour: Three tours start from this parking area. A 2⅓-mile marked ski loop heads east paralleling Highway 97 to the Blewett Pass Road then makes a looping return. You may also explore for several relatively peaceful miles up the Hovey Creek drainage. However, the best family and beginners' tour lies up the Iron Creek drainage.

For the first quarter of the tour the road parallels Iron Creek through a band of timber. Once the road crosses the creek the valley opens (a good place for picnicking).

Continuing up the valley, the road wanders along the creek, traversing small bands of trees. After 1 mile, Spur Road (9714)205 branches left following the West Fork for ⅓ mile to Spur Road (9714)112, which

Iron Creek Road

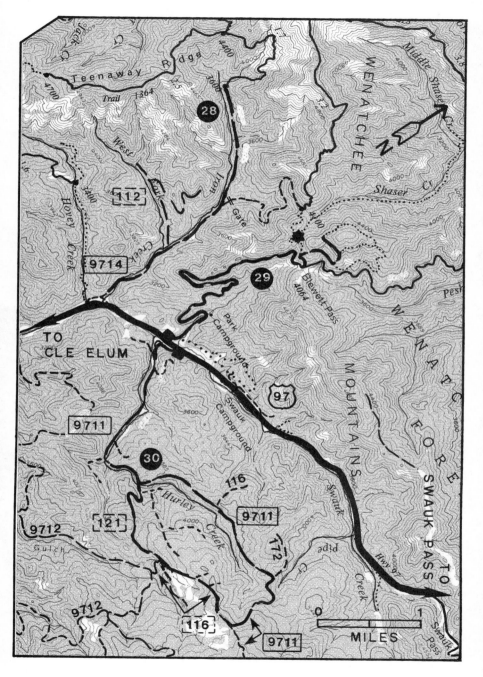

can be followed for a steep climb to the views from the 4,140-foot point on the ridge above.

Following the Iron Creek Road to the 2-mile mark, Spur Road (9714)113 branches right. This steep road climbs to a narrow pass (4,000 feet) 1 mile west of Blewett Pass.

Continuing up Iron Creek, a clearing at 2¾ miles suddenly reveals the end of the valley where the steep hillside rises to meet the summit of Teanaway Ridge. The road ends after 3 miles. Turn around and enjoy the glide back down the valley.

29 BLEWETT PASS

Blewett Pass

Class: *multiple use*
Rating: *more difficult*
Round trip: *8 miles*
Skiing time: *4 hours*
Elevation gain: *1,030 feet*
High point: *4,064 feet*
Best: *January–March*
Avalanche potential: *low*
Map: *Green Trails, Liberty No. 210*

Skiers' Trails

Class: *self-propelled*
Rating: *more difficult*
Round trip: *2 miles and more*
Skiing time: *1½ hours*
Elevation gain: *250 feet*
High point: *3,300 feet*
Best: *January–February*
Avalanche potential: *none*
Map: *Green Trails, Liberty No. 210*

Old names never die.

Highway 97 moved from Blewett Pass to Swauk Pass over 30 years ago, but the new road is still referred to as the Blewett Pass Highway. This tour takes you along the old Blewett Pass Highway to the real Blewett Pass. The tour is full of nostalgia—Model Ts used to chug and steam along here. Because old cars were not going fast, the old road twisted and turned its way upward, following contours of the hillside and doubling back on itself at switchbacks. It's frightening just how narrow the old two-lane was. Views from the sharp switchbacks sweep down Swauk River valley to Red Top Mountain and snow-topped Teanaway Ridge, and the descent down the old highway is a lot of fun, as long as you don't "lose your brakes" on the corners.

Access: Drive north on Highway 97 from Ellensburg or on Highway 970 from Cle Elum. At 7 miles from the junction of 97 and 970 pass Mineral Springs Resort. In 3 miles more find the old Blewett Pass Highway on the left (3,048 feet). There is usually space for about four cars to park.

Wenatchee Mountains viewed from Blewett Pass

Blewett Pass: Three trails start from the parking area, two for skiers and one for snowmobilers. The snowmobilers' trail goes to Blewett Pass; the blue-diamond Skiers' Trails do not. (Skiers' Trails are described below.)

To reach Blewett Pass, ski straight up from the parking area following the orange diamonds. (Do not attempt to follow the snowmobile tracks; they go everywhere.) After 30 feet you will reach an obvious road. Go right and ski up along the left side of a narrow clearing. Soon the timber closes in and the route is evident for the rest of the way to the pass.

The grade is gentle but steady. As elevation is gained, Red Top Mountain Lookout can be seen to the southwest and the flat top of Table Mountain to the southeast. At 1 mile the road divides; stay left and begin to switchback up the hillside.

At 4 miles, reach the 4,064-foot summit of Blewett Pass. Nothing is there now, but there used to be a small restaurant and, in the late 1930s, a rope-tow ski lift.

At the summit you are just a short distance from good views. Go left (west) and ski up a rough logging road, passing two spurs on the right. Stop at the edge of a long, open hillside and gaze down on the old highway below.

Skiers' Trails: If there are too many snowmobiles on the Blewett Pass Highway the two alternate tours may save your day. Both tours are fun romps through the forest on trails that gain very little elevation throughout their 2- and 2⅓-mile courses. Best of all, both trails make loops, so you won't have to keep dodging oncoming skiers.

The 2-mile trail begins on the right-hand side of the Blewett Pass Road. The first half of the trail parallels the Swauk Pass Highway. The trail winds a bit from one old skid road to another, so pay close attention to the blue diamonds marking the route. Shortly after passing Swauk Campground on the right, the route leaves the road, turns uphill, and bends back on itself.

The second half of the loop is considerably more challenging than the first. The return trip starts by wandering through the forest on a narrow trail then climbs up an old streambed to an abandoned logging road. The route follows the logging road down. Near the bottom, it veers back into the forest for a run across an open hillside back to the parking area.

The 2⅓-mile loop connects the Blewett Pass Road with the Iron Creek Road. Begin your loop by skiing up the Blewett Pass Road for 0.1 mile, then go left and switchback up a forested ridge. The trail dodges trees down to Iron Creek then returns paralleling Highway 97.

---

30 HURLEY CREEK LOOP

Class: multiple use
Rating: most difficult
Round trip: 11 miles
Skiing time: 5 hours
Elevation gain: 1,460 feet
High point: 4,500 feet
Best: mid-December–mid-March
Avalanche potential: low
Map: Green Trail, Liberty No. 210

Map on page 88

With its easy climb, fast descent, open meadows, ideal length, and looping configuration, the Hurley Creek Loop could be one of the premier ski tours in the Swauk Pass area. Unfortunately, this road is a popular snowmobile route. After skiing the loop, if you join us in

Hurley Rock

91

Mount Rainier seen from meadows on the Liberty–Beehive Road

believing that Hurley Creek should be included in the Pipe Creek no-motor area write to the Forest Service and let your views be heard.

Until Armageddon, ski the road early on weekends or on weekdays if you want to avoid the snowmobiles.

Access: Drive Highway 97 for 4.7 miles west from Swauk Pass (if coming from Highway 2) or 9.8 miles north from the intersection of Highways 97 and 970 (if coming from Interstate 90). Park on the south side of Highway 97 at the small Hurley Creek Road turnout (3,040 feet), just opposite the old Blewett Pass Highway (Tour 29).

The Tour: From the parking area, ski a slightly descending course along Road 9711 as it heads toward Hurley Creek. Near the creek the road makes an abrupt turn and enters the narrow valley where you will begin to climb. After ¾ mile the road crosses Hurley Creek and cuts through the first of two meadows (excellent camping for those so inclined).

Near the 2-mile point the valley makes an abrupt 90-degree turn to the north. The hills close in and the road cuts into the steep slope. You will reach Forest Service land after 2½ miles. At this point note Spur Road (9712)121, which joins the main road from the right and is the return leg of the loop.

Continuing up Hurley Creek, the road passes Hurley Rock at 3 miles and gains a small saddle between Pipe Creek and Hurley Creek after 5 miles.

At 6 miles (4,500 feet) reach the sloping shoulder of Swauk Ridge and go right on Spur Road (9712)116. Straight ahead is a beautiful meadow with an excellent view of Mount Rainier. Try a few turns here, and when you tire of playing slalom around the snowmobiles continue down Spur Road (9712)116 for another steep mile. Pass two roads on the right (both lead to summer cottages) and at the third road, No. (9712)121, turn right. Following the road, cross the ridge and prepare yourself for a straight drop down to Hurley Creek valley at 8½ miles. The final 2½ miles is a pleasant glide back to the car.

HIGHWAY 97

31 PIPE CREEK SNO-PARK

Class: groomed
Rating: most difficult
Round trip: 5–9½ miles
Skiing time: 3 or more hours
Elevation gain: 550 and up

High point: 4,350–4,958 feet
Best: mid-December–mid-March
Avalanche potential: low
Map: Green Trails, Liberty 210

Map on page 94

The Pipe Creek Sno-Park is like a breath of fresh winter in the center of one of the busiest freeways (for snowmobiles that is) in the state of Washington. The area accessed from the Pipe Creek Sno-Park is snowmobile-free, and skiers who come here can be assured of the chance to explore winter's tranquility in peace. Parents can bring their families without fear. Beginners can practice their skills with safety and dignity.

From the Sno-Park skiers have a choice of two trails: No. 141, which heads toward Swauk Pass, and No. 140 (the Pipe Creek Trail), which climbs steeply to views. Both of these trails can be turned into loops.

Access: From the west leave Interstate 90 at Exit 85 and head toward Wenatchee on Highway 970 to Highway 97. Continue north on Highway 97 for 13.1 miles to the Pipe Creek Road. The Sno-Park is on the right (3,500 feet). From the north, drive Highway 97 to Swauk Pass then head down the south side for 1.7 miles.

Trail 141: Heading north from the Sno-Park, this trail is rated *easiest*. It follows a logging road that parallels Highway 97 through forest and clearcuts. At the end of the first ½ mile the road divides; to the left a road (rated as *more difficult*) continues to parallel Highway 97 for the next 2 miles

93

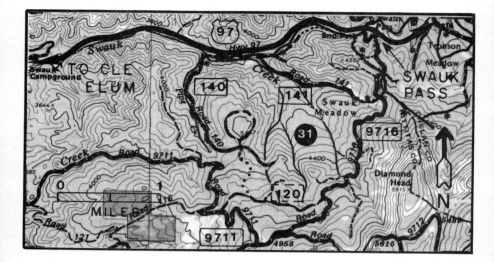

to the Swauk Pass Sno-Park (4,102 feet). Along the way the road ends and you must continue on a narrow trail. To the right Road 141 (*most difficult*) heads up to Swauk Meadow where you leave the road and continue the climb to Road 9716 on a trail marked with an occasional blue diamond. Once up on Road 9716, a *most difficult*, skier-only trail may be followed to Swauk Pass, making a 5½-mile loop, or you may connect the two trails by skiing Road 9716 (groomed for snowmobiles) north to Swauk Pass where you re-join the skier trail.

Pipe Creek Trail: The reason that this trail is rated *most difficult* becomes immediately apparent as you leave the Sno-Park and zoom down Road 140. The descent is steep and the road narrow for the first ⅛ mile of the tour. After crossing Swauk Creek the road begins to climb steadily, threading its way up a narrow canyon carved by Pipe Creek.

After a 2-mile climb you will reach a saddle and an intersection (4,300 feet). To the left is the Diamond View Loop, a mile-long trail that circum-navigates a forested hill and passes several fine viewpoints of Diamond Head and the Stuart Range. If the Diamond View Loop is your goal, your total trip mileage is 5 miles.

The Pipe Creek Trail continues on from the saddle, heading to the right (south). Before long your blue diamond–marked trail leaves maintained forest roads and heads out over skid roads and clearcuts. Although well marked, the trail's unexpected twists and turns make it difficult to follow. At the end of a mile you will reach an intersection (4,720 feet) with Road 120, called the Dunning Ranch Trail.

If you are looking for more adventure, go left (east) on the Dunning Ranch

Trail and follow it for 1 mile to Road 9716 (4,690 feet). Road 9716 is a nearly level and rather boring groomed snowmobile raceway that can be used to create several loops. If you go left (north) on Road 9716, you can loop back to the Pipe Creek Sno-Park via Swauk Meadow or Swauk Pass Trails for a total trip mileage of 8½ or 9½ miles, respectively.

If you head right (south) on Road 9716, you can cruise with the motorized sleds for ½ mile to a three-way intersection (4,958 feet). Go straight toward Liberty on Road 9712 and descend for ¼ mile then take a right on Hurley Creek Road No. 9711. Descend for another ½ mile then head to the right on Road 120 (the Dunning Ranch Trail). Ski across the open hillside for ⅛ mile to reconnect with the Pipe Creek Trail. Total trip mileage is 8¾ miles.

Diamond Head viewed from the Diamond View Loop

32 HUCKLEBERRY RIDGE

Class: *multiple use*
Rating: *most difficult*
Round trip: *8 miles or more*
Skiing time: *4 hours*
Elevation gain: *1,577 feet*

High point: *3,520 feet*
Best: *mid-December–March*
Avalanche potential: *low*
Map: *Green Trails, Greenwater*
No. 238

Map on page 96

Here is an area of almost unlimited potential for plodders, swooshers, racers, and trail breakers. This subalpine ridge sports miles and miles of crewcut hills as well as a mind-boggling network of roads. The results of all this human handiwork are far-flung views and roads to anywheresville. Meanwhile, skiers sure of their map-reading and skiing skills can skim across

95

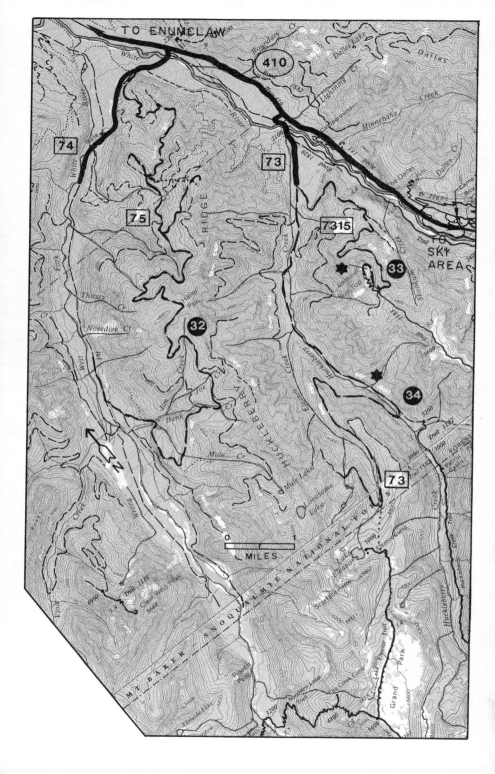

Skiers on Huckleberry Ridge Road

the clearcuts and develop their own paths along the ridge crest. Best of all, there are not that many snowmobiles in this area.

Access: Drive Highway 410 east 3.7 miles from the Greenwater General Store. Turn right on Forest Road 74 for 0.4 mile, then left on Road 75. Go less than 0.1 mile and make a right turn, still on Road 75 (1,943 feet), and head uphill to the snow. There is no Sno-Park here, so be sure to park out of the way of local traffic and driveways. When the snow level is at the valley floor, you may need to back-track a bit to find parking either near the White River bridge, just after the Highway 410 turnoff, or beyond the houses up West Fork Road No. 74. Be prepared for a few inconveniences here—after all the parking is free.

The Tour: Follow Road 75 as it climbs steadily through the forest for 2 miles. The first viewpoint, at 2¼ miles, looks out over the White River to Dallas Ridge. The next viewpoints look west over the West Fork White River.

At 3½ miles (3,300 feet), reach a four-way intersection. Skiers who feel droopy should turn right and then immediately turn right again. Climb steeply ⅛ mile to an old logging platform on the hilltop for a 360-degree view complete with Mount Rainier hovering above Huckleberry Ridge.

Perky skiers have a multitude of options. From the four-way intersection head up the clearcut hill for 1 mile. Cross three logging roads and at the fourth go left for views to the south and east.

The truly hyperactive may make a loop using Roads 75 and 74, skiing over 4,650-foot Haller Pass at 8 miles and returning along the West Fork White River for a 23-mile total. This loop is only possible during midwinter, when the snow is thick in the valley bottoms and four-wheel-drive vehicles are unable to rut the snow on the West Fork Road.

33 SUNTOP SNO-PARK

Huckleberry Creek

Class: *groomed*
Rating: *easiest*
Round trip: *9½ miles*
Skiing time: *4 hours*
Elevation gain: *700 feet*
High point: *2,900 feet*
Best: *mid-December–February*
Avalanche potential: *low*
Map: *Green Trails, Greenwater No. 238*

Suntop Lookout Road

Class: *groomed*
Rating: *most difficult*
Round trip: *10–11 miles*
Skiing time: *6 hours*
Elevation gain: *2,180 or 3,030 feet to summit*
High point: *4,420 or 5,279 at summit*
Best: *December–March*
Avalanche potential: *low to saddle, high to summit*
Map: *Green Trails, Greenwater No. 238*

Map on page 96

If we were rating Sno-Parks on a scale of 1 to 10, Suntop would receive a 20 because, not long ago, this entire area was overrun by snowmobiles. Skiers were harassed regularly, and backcountry campsites were blitzed by speeding machines. Thanks to the cooperation of the state-funded Sno-Park system and the Forest Service, this area has been turned into a true haven for skiers.

Two tours start from the Suntop Sno-Park. One tour follows a nearly level road along Huckleberry Creek and is ideal for families and beginners. The second tour climbs to a spectacular viewpoint on Suntop Mountain. Both tours receive regular grooming, eliminating the long slogs and trail breaking.

Access: Drive Highway 410 east from Enumclaw 24.2 miles and turn right on Huckleberry Creek Road No. 73. The road should be plowed for 1.4 miles to the Sno-Park (2,240 feet).

Huckleberry Creek: Ski around the gate to an intersection. Suntop Road is to the left. Continue straight ahead on a broad road that climbs gradually, alternating from forest to clearcuts. Watch for tracks in the snow as you ski. Spur roads abound and with them are numerous opportunities for exploration and snow play. At ¾ mile you will reach a major intersection; stay left on Road 73 and ski through beautiful old-growth forest. This congenial tour has numerous places that make excellent turnaround points, should small legs (or inexperienced ones) get tired.

Before long the road brushes near the creek. Cruise up Huckleberry Creek

Mount Rainier from a viewpoint below the summit of Suntop

valley then return to the creek again at about 1½ miles. Look for spur roads on the right if you would like to take a closer look at the water. The road wanders away from the creek then returns to it several more times.

At 4 miles the road crosses a narrow avalanche chute. The chute slides early in the season and at regular intervals thereafter. Be cautious here at all times and particularly so during or just after heavy precipitation. The grooming ends at 4¾ miles when Road 73 crosses Huckleberry Creek. The road continues on, climbing to the crest of Huckleberry Ridge (see Tour 34 for details).

Suntop Lookout Road: From the Sno-Park, ski around the gate to an intersection. Turn left, and head uphill on Road 7315. This road is groomed on one side only, allowing for a free descent lane for snowplowing or bombing on the other side.

The climb is steady and the road slips rapidly through a green-and-white patchwork of forest and clearcut, passing an occasional side road. By the end of the first mile you will reach the first of many viewpoints over the White River valley and east to Dallas Ridge. Near the 2-mile point, Spur Road (7315)301 branches to the right, offering views over Huckleberry Creek, and ½ mile farther Spur Road (7315)401 branches to the left, ending in a clearcut overlooking the White River valley. No need to worry about accidentally taking the wrong road, the Suntop Road is the only one that is groomed.

At about 5 miles, the road makes a final switchback to the forested 4,420-foot saddle below Suntop. The groomed trail ends here, and on most days so does the tour. Between the saddle and the summit, the road crosses several extremely dangerous avalanche slopes. Most of the views seen from the summit can be found by continuing straight across the saddle for ½ mile to excellent vantage points of Mount Rainier.

For those choosing to continue to the summit of Suntop despite the very real hazard of avalanches, go right and follow the road up from the saddle to the edge of the trees, then ski (climbing skins are a must) or hike directly up the south rib to the lookout, following the summer trail. Do not ski the road beyond the edge of the trees, as both the east and west sides of the summit pyramid are extremely hazardous. After heavy snowfalls no route to the summit is safe and skiers should turn back at the saddle.

Note: When there is insufficient snow at the Sno-Park (early or late season, or low-snow years), parking will be moved 2.1 miles up Road 7315.

34 GRAND PARK

Class: self-propelled
Rating: backcountry
Round trip: 21 miles
Skiing time: 2–3 days
Elevation gain: 3,540 feet

High point: 5,640 feet
Best: January–March
Avalanche potential: moderate
Maps: Green Trails, Greenwater No. 238
    and Mt. Rainier East No. 270

Map on page 96

As a rule most winter tours on the flanks of Mount Rainier National Park are strictly reserved for competent ski mountaineers. But most rules have their exceptions, and strong skiers with backcountry skis, moderate skills, and a couple of days to spare can reach the wide meadows of Grand Park, just a stone's throw from the northeast base of "The Mountain."

Camping on a clear night in Grand Park in full view of The Mountain is a once-in-a-lifetime experience, and skiing across the broad meadow under a full moon is truly memorable.

Access: Drive to the Suntop Sno-Park (2,240 feet; see Tour 33).

The Tour: From the Sno-Park follow the groomed Road 73 (the Huckleberry Creek Trail; see Tour 33 for details). The road starts off as a nearly level

Grand Park and Mount Rainier from Scarface

cruise. After a mile in the trees the road enters clearcuts in Huckleberry Creek valley and parallels the creek. At 4 miles cross a narrow avalanche chute. The chute slides early in the season and at regular intervals thereafter. Be cautious here at all times and particularly so during or just after heavy precipitation.

At 4¾ miles the road crosses Huckleberry Creek (2,960 feet), where the grooming ends. From the crossing the road gains elevation quickly for

1½ miles, then, at the 3,680-foot level, bends sharply into the Eleanor Creek drainage. The grade now gentles. After another 2 miles the road bends sharply to cross Eleanor Creek (4,480 feet). Leave the road and enter the forest left (east) of Eleanor Creek. Head straight ahead to the trees and in a few yards you will cross the park boundary.

The next 3 miles is an unmarked backcountry route through the trees to Grand Park that requires a good map. From the National Park boundary head south–southwest, keeping to the left of the small valley between Scarface to the west and the ridge to the east. If you come to Lake Eleanor, you have gone too far to the west and need to head east for ¼ mile before skiing a southwest course up an ascending bench for the final 1¼ miles to Grand Park. You may spot blazes and other signs of a summer trail from Lake Eleanor on. When the bench ends, climb steeply for 200 feet to the flat meadowland that is Grand Park (5,600 feet) with broad views of Carbon, Winthrop, and Emmons Glaciers. After your eyes weary of our state's greatest heap of snow, look away, to lower peaks, to snow-hung trees, and to the critter tracks on the glistening white plain.

HIGHWAY 410—WEST

35 BUCK CREEK TOUR

Class: self-propelled
Rating: more difficult
Round trip: 10 miles
Skiing time: 5 hours
Elevation gain: 1,800 feet

High point: 4,400 feet
Best: mid-December–March
Avalanche potential: moderate
Map: Green Trails, Greenwater No. 238

We headed out to find a tour in the White River valley away from snowmobiles and we found a real gem at Buck Creek. This area is a wintering ground for elk and is closed from November through April to all motorized use. On this tour you can count on seeing elk sign (tracks winding up and down the hillsides) as well as views over the White River valley. The tour follows a road for 5 miles, winding in and out of the Buck Creek drainage, ending at the top of a clearcut on a flank of Fawn Ridge. However, you do not need to ski the entire distance to enjoy the views, which are as good at the 1½-mile point as they are from the top.

Access: Drive to Enumclaw and then head east on Highway 410 to Greenwater. From the Greenwater General Store continue south 11.5 miles, then turn right opposite the large Forest Service "Organizational Sites" sign. When the snow is thick on the valley floor you can park next to

Buck Creek Road

the intersection; otherwise, cross the White River on Buck Creek Road No. 7160. After 0.2 mile reach an intersection; stay with Road 7160, which is on the right. In 0.9 mile a large sign marks the entrance to Buck Creek Church Camp (2,600 feet). If there is room to park on the left side of the road, just before the sign, do so; if not, drive the 0.9 mile back to the intersection, park, and return on skis along the edge of the road.

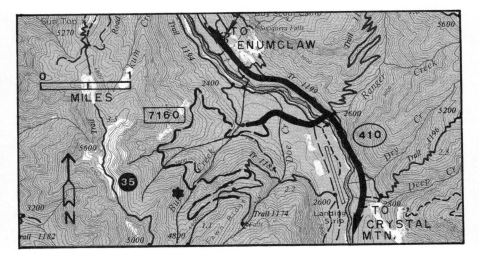

The Tour: The Buck Creek Road tour begins directly in front of the church camp sign and heads across the valley floor for ⅛ mile before starting to climb. A spur road joins on the left at the first switchback. At ½ mile the road divides (no road signs); take the right fork to cross Buck Creek, then climb into an open clearcut and views. To the east Snoquera Falls makes its breathtaking plunge down a broad expanse of cliffs; south lie the snowcapped summits of Castle Mountain, Norse Peak, and Crystal Mountain, and directly below is the forested White River valley.

The road climbs across the clearcut, switchbacks, then heads over the top of the clearing. At 2 miles is a gate; ski around it and continue the climb. At 3¼ miles the road divides (this should be the turnaround point if there has been any recent snowfall). Take the right fork and descend across an avalanche slope then cross Buck Creek for a second time before resuming the climb. The road enters a large clearcut at 4 miles, and the final mile of the tour is spent switchbacking up to the logging platform at the top of the clearing.

36 CORRAL PASS

Class: *self-propelled*
Rating: *most difficult*
Round trip: *10 miles*
Skiing time: *6 hours*
Elevation gain: *3,000*

High point: *5,700 feet*
Best: *December–mid-May*
Avalanche potential: *low*
Maps: *Green Trails, Mt. Rainier East
No. 270, Greenwater No. 238, and
Lester No. 239*

Here's a day tour for the entire snow season—be it late fall, midwinter, or early spring. But don't limit your explorations of the Corral Pass environs to day use only. High ridge tops and snowy bowls abound in the area, making the pass a fine overnight destination as well.

The Corral Pass Road starts at 2,700 feet and climbs, and climbs, and then climbs some more, gaining 3,000 feet in just 5 miles. Start at the bottom with a fast stride and hope that the momentum will carry on to the top.

Access: Drive Highway 410 from Enumclaw east through Greenwater and on. Note the mileage as you pass the Four Season Mountain Resort and continue east for 0.5 mile to Corral Pass Road No. 7174 located on the left-hand side of the highway. In midwinter parking is difficult. There is no parking on the Corral Pass Road unless the snow level lies above 3,000 feet, well above the cluster of private cabins. If the snow level is near the valley floor, you must drive on to the Silver Springs Sno-Park—located 1.2 miles beyond the Corral Pass Road on the Crystal Mountain access road—and walk back.

The Tour: When the snow level is down to Highway 410, walk from the Sno-Park back to the Corral Pass Road. Head up this road for ½ mile past vacation cabins to an intersection. Skiing will start here (2,850 feet). Continue straight on Road 7174 and climb. Steep switchback follows steep switchback until you arrive at an open meadow below Castle Mountain (5,300 feet) after 4¼ miles. If time allows, ski the delightful slopes at the south and southwest end of the meadow on an offshoot ridge of Castle Mountain.

Corral Pass is reached at 5 miles (5,700 feet). Ski right at the pass to find a large open area, parking lot, summertime picnic area, and winter campsite. For an alternative campsite, continue along the road to Corral Pass Campground, located on a small, frozen stream running through the trees.

For the best views ski north from the pass to Mutton Mountain. From Corral Pass ski straight east up the hillside and through a band of trees. At the first open area turn north and climb up to the ridge top. Continue north over several small rolls along the ridge until it drops off in front of your skis. Descend west to a saddle, then climb to rounded Mutton Mountain (5,900

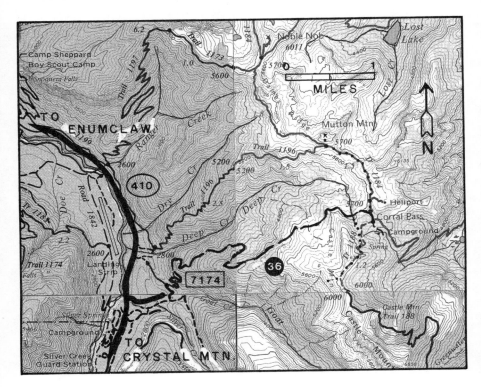

Campsite on ridge between Corral Pass and Mutton Mountain; Mount Rainier in distance

feet). If you got this far without noticing the view, now is the time to feast your eyes. Mount Rainier fills the horizon to the southwest, while Mount Stuart and the Snoqualmie-area peaks rise to the east. Finally, Noble Knob to the north and Castle Mountain to the south scratch the sky as well.

37 NORSE PEAK

Bullion Basin

Class: self-propelled
Rating: mountaineer
Round trip: 4 miles
Skiing time: 3 hours
Elevation gain: 1,500 feet
High point: 5,700 feet
Best: mid-December–May
Avalanche potential: moderate
Map: Green Trails, Bumping Lake
  No. 271

Norse Peak

Class: self-propelled
Rating: mountaineer
Round trip: 9 miles
Skiing time: 6 hours
Elevation gain: 2,656 feet
High point: 6,856 feet
Best: mid-December–May
Avalanche potential: high
Map: Green Trails, Bumping Lake
  No. 271

Bullion Basin and Norse Peak are perfect examples of the challenging backcountry skiing found in the Crystal Mountain area. The mountains rise straight out of the valley floor and avalanches commonly sweep their slopes.

Skiers unable to assess avalanche danger are playing a game of Russian roulette as soon as they leave the groomed area, but experienced skiers who know when the slopes are safe can knock the needle off the fun meter, cranking tight turns down the long bowls.

Bullion Basin is a mere scoop cut into rugged talus. Sheltered by shady nooks and crannies, the snow stays light and powdery here long after it has elsewhere turned to corn or melted. Do not ski above Bullion Basin except when the snow pack is very stable.

Norse Peak lies above Bullion Basin, above timberline, and above the avalanches that plague the steep hillsides around it. Start the tour early so you'll have ample time to sample the bowls just beyond Norse Peak.

Access: Drive Highway 410 east from Enumclaw to the gated entrance of Mount Rainier National Park. Turn left and drive to the end of the Crystal Mountain Road and the downhill skiers' parking area (4,200 feet). Register with the Ski Patrol and get the latest update on avalanche conditions before you start.

The Tour: Bullion Basin and Norse Peak start from the upper parking area. From the chapel don your climbing skins and climb around the

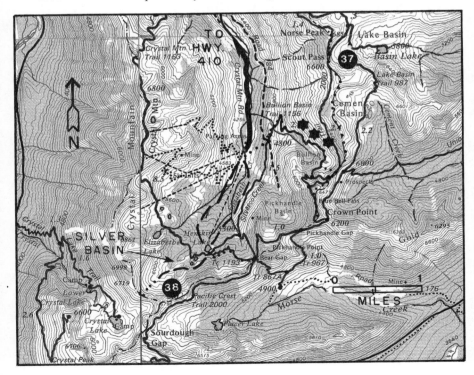

Skier on route to Bullion Basin

children's ski area. Continue up the Gold Hills area, staying close to the trees so as not to interfere with the downhill runs. Once at the top of the lifts, continue on up to the old Mine-to-Market Road. Staying well to the left of the cabins, find where the road switchbacks near the top of the lift. Go left through the switchback at 4,800 feet to find Bullion Basin Trail No. 1156. The trail is hidden under the snow and difficult to follow, so plot a course that takes you on a northwest traverse to reach the creek from Bullion Basin at 4,860 feet.

At this point there are two routes that lead on to the basin and peak. The trail heads over to the left side of the valley where a steep jeep road cuts an obvious path, but this area is extremely avalanche-prone and should mostly be avoided. The safest route is to the right, climbing to the top of a sparsely timbered knob on the south side of the creek. Keep right along the south side of the valley in level terrain until the slope steepens, then enter dense timber. At 5,500 feet cross the first of several small clearings. Bullion Basin lies only 200 vertical feet above, but it requires ¼ mile of climbing through sparse forest on either side of a prominent knob to reach it. Above the knob climb through a final fringe of timber to the bowl at the head of Bullion Basin.

To reach Norse Peak follow the edge of the timber north around the entrance of the bowl, then head up a sparsely timbered ridge to a 6,700-foot knoll. In the next 1½ miles ski over the knoll and head north along the ridge overlooking Cement Basin, over a second 6,700-foot knoll, and along the ridge at the top of Lake Basin, to the 6,856-foot summit of Norse Peak.

If time and weather permit, ski the sweeping slopes of Lake Basin and Big Crow Basin on the east side of the peak.

38 SILVER BASIN

Silver Basin

Class: self-propelled
Rating: backcountry
Round trip: 4½ miles
Skiing time: 4 hours
Elevation gain: 1,800 feet
High point: 6,000 feet
Best: mid-December–May
Avalanche potential: low
Map: Green Trails, Bumping Lake
    No. 271

Bear Gap

Class: self-propelled
Rating: backcountry
Round trip: 4½ miles
Skiing time: 4 hours
Elevation gain: 1,682 feet
High point: 5,882 feet
Best: mid-December–March
Avalanche potential: low
Map: Green Trails, Bumping Lake
    No. 271

Map on page 107

Completely hidden from the noise and hard-packed slopes of the Crystal Mountain Ski Area, Silver Basin lies secluded by steep mountain walls in a fairy-tale world of winter beauty. Deep, fluffy powder often covers the small lakes, open meadows, and hillsides, offering a variety of skiing from serene gliding to mad downhill thrills. Bear Gap gives untracked snow and views to corniced ridges and the snowbound Cascade Mountains.

Access: Park at the Crystal Mountain Ski Area parking lot (see Tour 37) (4,200 feet). Be sure to register with the Ski Patrol and check on avalanche conditions before starting out.

Silver Basin: The first 1,000 feet to Silver Basin can be gained by skiing up the Quicksilver Run (climbing skins will help) then branching left on to Boondoggle. You may also buy a one-ride ticket up the Quicksilver Chair (No. 4). From the chair top (5,420 feet), a Sno-Cat often sets a track to Silver Basin. If no track can be seen, head southwest toward Hen Skin Lake, reached in ½ mile. Circle the east shore and proceed west, continually gaining elevation. Another long ¼ mile will take you past two more small, snow-covered lakes to an open meadow (5,580 feet). Follow this long clearing southwest into Silver Basin. The wide-open slopes above are prime cross-country downhilling terrain. If snow conditions are stable, ski up to the ridge for a breathtaking view of Mount Rainier.

The return retraces the route to the top of Chair 4 then takes one of the downhill runs to the bottom. The Tinkerbell Run to the left (west) of Quicksilver is suggested because it usually is the least mogulled.

Bear Gap: From the parking lot ski up the Boondoggle Run or ride the Quicksilver Chair and ski to the southeast end of Boondoggle (5,460 feet). Head southeast in untracked snow for a long ¾ mile, aiming for the lowest saddle in the ridge, which is Bear Gap (5,882 feet). Cross the gap to views south and east, the perfect lunch spot on a sunny day. The return to the top of Quicksilver is a long, rolling downhill run.

Skiing the excellent snow near Bear Gap

39 SILVER CREEK SKI ROUTE

Viewpoint

Class: *multiple use*
Rating: *easiest*
Round trip: *10 miles*
Skiing time: *5 hours*
Elevation gain: *1,140 feet*
High point: *3,880 feet*
Best: *January–mid-February*
Avalanche potential: *low*
Map: *Green Trails, Mt. Rainier East No. 270*

White River Campground

Class: *multiple use*
Rating: *easiest*
Round trip: *23 miles*
Skiing time: *2 days*
Elevation gain: *1,742 feet*
High point: *4,232 feet*
Best: *mid-December–March*
Avalanche potential: *low*
Map: *Green Trails, Mt. Rainier East No. 270*

Map on page 112

The Silver Creek Ski Route offers winter access to the White River area of Mount Rainier National Park. The route follows Highway 410 from the Crystal Mountain turnoff to Mather Junction then heads deeper into the park to end in old-growth forest at White River Campground. The tour passes through an amazing winter wonderland of snow-laced trees, ice-covered creeks, and unexpected vistas. Elk inhabit this area throughout the winter and your ski tracks are often potholed with their hoofprints.

Despite the charm of this area, the tour completely lacks any kind of wilderness feel. For the first 4 miles half the road is plowed so that the snowplows can reach their maintenance buildings. The other half of the road must be shared by skiers and snowmobiles. (Snowmobile use is not heavy but you will probably encounter several on a weekend.)

Access: Drive east on Highway 410 to the end of the plowing at the National Park boundary. Turn left on the Crystal Mountain access road for 100 feet, then go right to enter the Silver Springs Sno-Park (2,740 feet).

Viewpoint: Locate the information board on the northwest end of the Sno-Park and ski into the trees. Traverse southwest 1,000 feet to meet Highway 410 at the entrance arch to Mount Rainier National Park. Ski under the arch then up the road under a dense forest cover. The highway heads up the White River valley; however, you will ski a mile before actually seeing the river.

The road climbs gradually through old-growth timber. Elk tracks are everywhere. If you should happen to be on this route at sundown or in the dark, use caution to avoid running into these large animals.

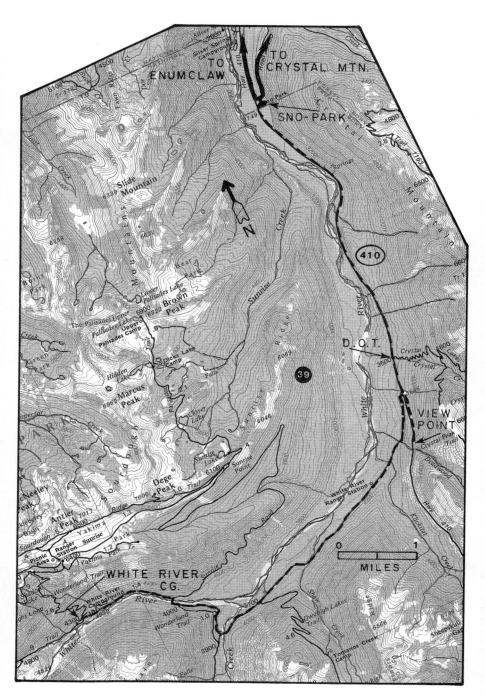

TO ENUMCLAW

TO CRYSTAL MTN.

SNO-PARK

Silver Springs Campground

Slide Mountain

Bear Park

The Palisades
Lower Palisades Lake
Upper Palisades Lake
Upper Palisades Camp
Brown Peak

Sunrise Ridge

Dicks Lake Camp

Hidden Lake

Marcus Peak

Clover Lake

39

Sunrise Lake

Sunrise Point

Dege Peak

White River Ranger Station

410

D.O.T.

Crystal

VIEW POINT

Crystal Peak Trail

Deadwood

Hwy 410

Klickitat Creek

Negley Peak

Webley's Basin

Antler Peak

Ranger Station

Picnic Area

Sunrise

Yakima Park Tr.

Sunrise

WHITE RIVER CG.

Wonderland Trail

White River Campground

Wonderland Trail

River

Owyhigh Lakes

Tomanos Creek Camp

Sheepskull Gap

0   1
MILES

Giant icicles adorn hillside along the Silver Creek Ski Route

Near the 2-mile point the road carves its way across a steep bank with an excellent view of the White River. The climb steepens, not drastically, but just enough to offer an enjoyable glide on the way back. At 4 miles pass the Crystal Lakes Trail on the left and, a few feet beyond, pass the Department of Transportation maintenance buildings on the right. Continue up the road, passing the gravel pile before reaching 3,686-foot Mather Junction at 4½ miles from the Sno-Park.

When, and only when, the snow pack is stable, continue on up Highway 410. At the upper end of the intersection ski right past the red signs that inform snowmobiles that they must stop and prepare to enjoy a final ½ mile in peace. The viewpoint is a broad turnout located on the right-hand side of the road (3,840 feet). On a cloudy day you may wonder why you skied all the way to this point; on a clear day, however, the view over the White River valley to Mount Rainier will be explanation enough.

White River Campground: From the Silver Springs Sno-Park ski up Highway 410 for 4½ miles to Mather Junction as described above. From the junction go right on the Sunrise Road and descend for the next mile. At 5½ miles the road crosses Klickitat Creek (3,460 feet) and resumes a very gradual climb. The White River Ranger Station and entrance booths are passed at 5¾ miles.

The next 2 miles are spent cruising west. At 7 miles the road crosses Shaw Creek. The Owyhigh Lakes Trailhead is passed at 7¾ miles. Near the 8½-mile point the road crosses Fryingpan Creek and soon after passes the Wonderland Trail. Burrowing through the old-growth forest the road heads around the base of Goat Island Mountain then crosses the White River at 10 miles. Beyond the bridge the road divides—go left and continue up the White River valley on a narrow road that reaches the campground at 11½ miles.

Pick your campsite carefully. Avoid camping under large trees that might dump snow or drop old branches on your tent in the middle of the night. (No drinking water or services are available at the campground.)

40 CHINOOK PASS AND NACHES PEAK

Chinook Pass

Class: self-propelled
Rating: most difficult
Round trip: 4 miles
Skiing time: 2 hours
Elevation gain: 832 feet
High point: 5,432 feet
Best: November–December
Avalanche potential: low
Map: Green Trails, Mt. Rainier East No.270

Naches Peak (false summit)

Class: self-propelled
Rating: backcountry
Round trip: 7 miles
Skiing time: 4 hours
Elevation gain: 1,760 feet
High point: 6,360 feet
Best: November–December
Avalanche potential: moderate
Maps: Green Trails, Mt. Rainier East No. 270 and Bumping Lake No. 271

Skiing in the Chinook Pass–Naches Peak area starts with the first major snowstorms to hit the Cascades. There is great fun to be had challenging the open bowls leading to Dewey Lakes or simply taking in incomparable views of Mount Rainier.

The skiing season around Chinook Pass starts and ends early. Beginning as soon as Highway 410 is closed over the pass, it ends when 4,694-foot Cayuse Pass is snowed in, usually by mid- to late December. In late spring there is often another week or two of skiing before the snowplows come to end the fun.

Mount Rainier from a shoulder of Naches Peak

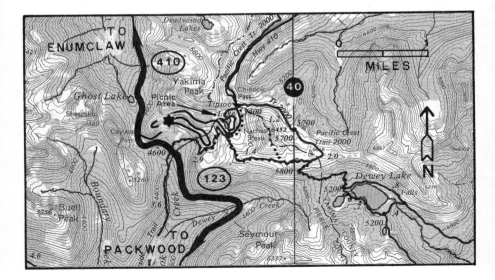

Note: Do not even consider skiing up Highway 410 to Cayuse or Chinook Pass during the midwinter months. The road crosses several steep avalanche slide areas, making travel extremely hazardous.

Access: From Enumclaw drive Highway 410 for 41 miles to the summit of Cayuse Pass. Cross the pass and park in one of the turnouts just beyond.

Chinook Pass: On skis, contour through the trees below the Chinook Pass Highway heading southeast for ¼ to ½ mile, before heading uphill. Be sure to stay well away from the highway and in the protection of the trees. After ½ mile of climbing steeply, the forest route bisects the highway where it makes a sharp switchback north. Follow the road to reach 5,294-foot Tipsoo Lake and excellent views of Mount Rainier from the snowbound bowl. The road can be followed for the final ½ mile to Chinook Pass. Skiing beyond the pass is not recommended, as the steep slopes are avalanche-prone.

Naches Peak (false summit): From Tipsoo Lake, follow the road another 500 feet and climb to the smaller, upper Tipsoo Lake. Then ski south up a lightly timbered ridge. When the open slope below a ridge running west from the false summit of Naches Peak is reached, traverse west to gain that ridge, avoiding the cornices above. Once on the ridge crest, follow its south side to the false summit of Naches Peak, the 6,360-foot chief viewpoint of the trip. From the false summit, ski out to Dewey Lakes or just be satisfied with a great run back to the car. Sections of the descent are steep so be sure your turns and stopping ability are in good form.

MOUNT RAINIER NATIONAL PARK

41 MOWICH LAKE

Class: *self-propelled*
Rating: *more difficult*
Round trip: *11 miles*
Skiing time: *6 hours*
Elevation gain: *1,410 feet*

High point: *4,960 feet*
Best: *March–April*
Avalanche potential: *low*
Map: *Green Trails, Mt. Rainier West No. 269*

Nestled in the forest at the base of glacier-wrapped Mount Rainier, Mowich Lake is an excellent tour for a day or a weekend outing. While the area has prime skiing throughout the winter, access problems make it best to leave this tour for the spring when the roads are snow-free at least to the park boundary.

Access: Drive Highway 410 to Buckley. At the west end of town turn south on Highway 165 for 10.5 miles, passing through Wilkeson and crossing the

Skiers on route to Mowich Lake

Fairfax Bridge over the Carbon River. At the junction beyond the bridge take the right fork to Mowich Lake. A "Road Closed" sign here indicates the road receives no winter plowing or maintenance. The first 1.3 miles of pavement is followed by 10 miles on dirt. The boundary of Mount Rainier National Park and the start of the tour are reached at 11.3 miles (3,550 feet).

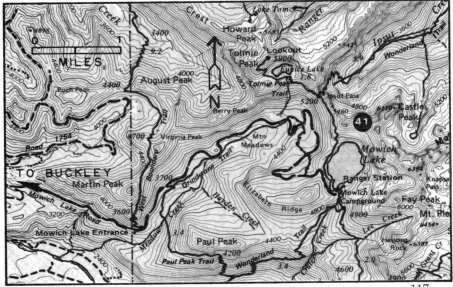

The Tour: There are two ways to ski to the lake. You can either follow the road for 5½ miles or ski a 4½-mile road-and-trail combination suited for skiers with *backcountry* skills. The two routes begin together on the Mowich Lake Road.

Ski the road through dense forest, passing the Paul Peak Picnic Area ¾ mile from the park boundary. The climb is gentle but steady to the end of the valley. At 3 miles (4,280 feet), the road makes a long curve to the south. Here the trail leaves the road to ascend a shallow gully ¼ mile before recrossing the road. The second section of trail climbs along the left of a small creek for ½ mile before intersecting the road again (4,640 feet). The third and final ½-mile section of trail is the steepest, rejoining the road at 4,920 feet. Once back on the road (if you ever got off it), turn left and ski to the west side of Mowich Lake (4,960 feet). If in doubt about the trail, stay on the road. (The Park Service may start marking the trail in years to come.)

Campsites are found at the road-end on the south side of the lake and viewpoints on the west side. For vistas, ski left from the high point of the road and head up a forested ridge until Mount Rainier comes in sight over the lake. Watch the thundering spring avalanches cascade down the sheer rock face of Willis Wall.

MOUNT RAINIER NATIONAL PARK

42 SEATTLE PARK AND RUSSELL GLACIER

Class: self-propelled
Rating: backcountry to Seattle Park, mountaineer to Russell Glacier
Round trip: 16 miles to Seattle Park
Skiing time: 2–3 days
Elevation gain: 3,600 feet

High point: 6,400 feet
Best: May–June
Avalanche potential: low
Map: Green Trails, Mt. Rainier West No. 269

The north-facing slopes of Mount Rainier offer superb spring skiing long after the south-side snows are hard and sun-cupped. Of the numerous destinations on the north side, Seattle Park is one of the easiest to reach and provides the most rewarding views and skiing.

Above the snow-covered meadows and the clumps of trees at Seattle Park lies a telemarking paradise—2 miles and over 3,000 vertical feet of rolling terrain terminating at the base of Ptarmigan Ridge and the Mowich Face. The skiing is not difficult here, but the tour above Seattle Park should be reserved for skiers with mountaineering experience. Weather around Mount Rainier changes suddenly and routefinding skills are essential when the miles of nondescript slopes dissolve into a white soup.

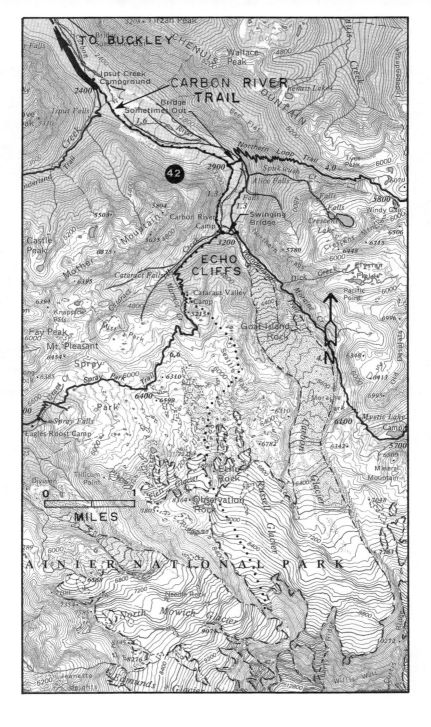

Skiers' camp in upper Seattle Park

Access: Drive to the Carbon River Entrance of Mount Rainier National Park, register at the entrance station, then drive to the end of the road at Ipsut Creek Campground (2,400 feet).

The Tour: Ski or hike up the valley on the Carbon River Trail staying on the west side of the river for 3 miles. The trail passes a small camp area then crosses Cataract Creek on a log bridge to reach a junction at 3,000 feet. Turn right and head up the Cataract Creek valley on the trail if it can be found. If the trail is under the snow, choose a course between Cataract Creek and Echo Cliffs on the hillside above. Once past Echo Cliffs (about ¾ mile up Cataract Creek, elevation 4,000 feet), you will encounter Marmot Creek. Follow it up the steep hillside to its headwaters at timberline and the base of Seattle Park.

Seattle Park extends upward for another ¾ mile, and outstanding views of Mount Rainier and Willis Wall abound. Little exploration is required to find an outstanding campsite, but it is difficult to determine which site is positively the most scenic.

Mountaineering skiers continuing higher will discover myriad possibilities.

Head south from Seattle Park past Echo Rock, then onto the glacier itself. There are excellent slopes on Russell Glacier all the way up to 9,600 feet, before the terrain steepens. Avoid skiing too far to the east, however, where the slopes steepen, crevasses exist, and falling rocks and ice can ruin your skis and other things.

To the west and north you will find a long succession of exhilarating ski slopes down into Spray Park. In years of low snowfall, stay off Russell Glacier in June and ski these broad snow slopes instead.

MOUNT RAINIER NATIONAL PARK

43 REFLECTION LAKES

Class: self-propelled
Rating: more difficult
Round trip: 3 miles
Skiing time: 2 hours
Elevation gain: 538 feet

High point: 5,100 feet
Best: January–mid-April
Avalanche potential: low
Map: Green Trails, Mt. Rainier East No. 270

Map on page 122

In summer the Reflection Lakes mirror colorful flowers of the surrounding meadows below the images of the gleaming white glaciers of Mount Rainier. Most visitors pause briefly to click cameras and drive on. In winter, however, though the little snow-covered lakes reflect nothing but the sun, they are the objective of numerous day trips and overnight outings.

Access: From the Nisqually Entrance to Mount Rainier National Park, follow the Paradise Road to Narada Falls Viewpoint (4,572 feet). In winter a large parking area is plowed for skiers and the warming hut–restroom facility is kept open.

The Tour: From the parking lot the aim is to gain Stevens Canyon Road on the top of the steep hill straight ahead. Don't attempt to climb directly up the open slope behind the warming hut, the avalanche hazard makes this approach dangerous. The safe way is to start near the warming hut and stay in the forest, climbing the left side of the open slope. The farther to the left, the easier the grade.

Once on Stevens Canyon Road go to the right. Before long the road divides; if the snow is stable, stay right and follow the road across the windswept hillside above the warming hut followed by a mile of easy going to the lakes. The road should never be skied when conditions are unstable. If in doubt, ask a ranger before starting. If there is a possibility of avalanches,

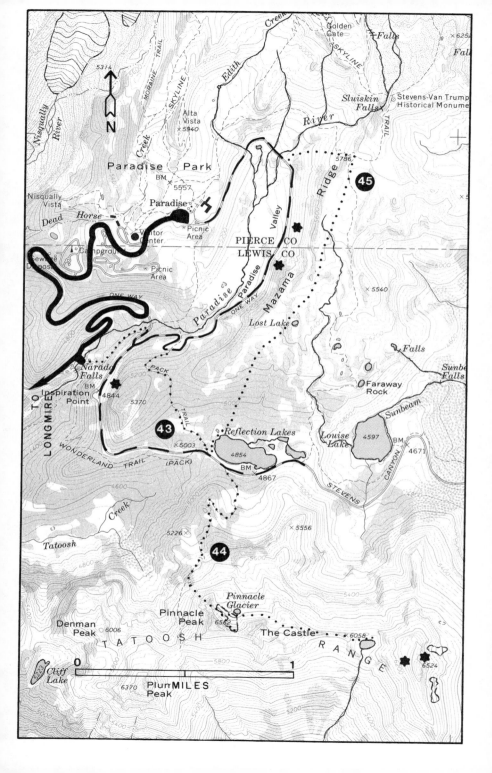

Castle (left) and Pinnacle (right) Peaks from Reflection Lakes

go left at the intersection and ski up the old Paradise Valley Road. After ¼ mile go right on a well-signed but very steep and narrow ski trail that climbs over Mazama Ridge (5,100 feet) then descends back to Stevens Canyon Road. Once down, ski left along the road ¼ mile to the largest Reflection Lake (4,854 feet).

At the lake, an obvious option is to wander the snowy meadows. Another is to visit Louise Lake. To do so, continue on the road, passing the two main Reflection Lakes. At the head of Stevens Canyon the road makes a broad bend and descends a lower bench and Louise Lake. You may also leave the road at the head of the bend and descend the open slope to the lake (4,597 feet).

Other popular tours in the lakes area are the Tatoosh Range (Tour 44) and to Paradise via Mazama Ridge (Tour 45).

44 TATOOSH RANGE

Class: *self-propelled*
Rating: *backcountry*
Round trip: *5 miles*
Skiing time: *4 hours*
Elevation gain: *1,432 feet*

High point: *6,000 feet*
Best: *January–April*
Avalanche potential: *moderate*
Map: *Green Trails, Mt. Rainier East No. 270*

Map on page 122

As viewed from a small saddle on the side of Castle Peak in the Tatoosh Range, the enormous bulk of Mount Rainier fills the entire northern horizon. Below lies a basin whose deep snow generally is much drier than that across the valley at Paradise, and the steep slopes are ideal for telemarking.

Access: From the Nisqually Entrance to Mount Rainier National Park, drive to the Narada Falls Viewpoint parking area (4,572 feet).

The Tour: Ski to Reflection Lakes (4,854 feet) (see Tour 43). Skiers who have hiked this area in the summer are familiar with the two trails from the Reflection Lakes vicinity up into the Tatoosh Range, the Bench and Snow Lakes Trail and the Pinnacle Saddle Trail. Both are highly avalanche-prone in winter. There is, however, a relatively avalanche-free entry to the Tatoosh Range via Castle Saddle.

Ski Stevens Canyon Road halfway around the first Reflection Lake. At a convenient point leave the road and start uphill into a big basin with a steep headwall. The avalanche-free route follows the Pinnacle Saddle Trail up the right side of the basin to the fringe of trees atop a rib. Once on the rib, leave the trail and head up through the open forest at the rib's crest. When the rib steepens and becomes impassable, cross the top of the headwall and climb into another big basin between Pinnacle Peak on the right and The Castle on the left. Follow the treeline on the left of the basin. When the trees end, climb the last 200 feet of steep open slopes on the east side of Castle to the crest of the Tatoosh Range (6,000 feet).

Look south to the three southern giants—the dark, steaming mass of Mount St. Helens, the sharp summit of Mount Hood, and the rounded mass of Mount Adams. All three are dwarfed by massive Mount Rainier to the north.

For most skiers the saddle is enough. However, those who wish to go farther (when the snow is stable) can cross to the south side of the saddle and head east to the next small hill, staying well away from the corniced summit. Continue to a saddle (6,000 feet) below Unicorn Glacier. This is a

Mount Rainier dominates the horizon along the route to Castle Saddle

good turnaround; beyond, the avalanche potential is high. When the snow is very stable, good skiing may be found in the steep bowls on the south side of the ridge.

45 MAZAMA RIDGE

Class: *self-propelled*
Rating: *backcountry*
Round trip: *6 miles*
Skiing time: *4 hours*
Elevation gain: *900 feet in,*
900 feet out

High point: *5,700 feet*
Best: *January–mid-May*
Avalanche potential: *moderate*
Map: *Green Trails, Mt. Rainier East*
No. 270

Map on page 122

The snowy meadows of Mazama Ridge offer excellent skiing amidst some of the most breathtaking scenery of Mount Rainier National Park. The meadows and views from the ridge crest can be the very satisfying objective of the tour, or you may ski a challenging loop down the ridge to Reflection Lakes and return via an easy cruise up Stevens Canyon Road.

Skiing the meadows on Mazama Ridge

Mazama Ridge is fun in most weather and snow conditions and with careful navigation can even be skied in a whiteout; however, this is a backcountry tour without any markings for skiers to follow. Luckily, this is a popular trip and there are usually ski tracks to follow. Sections of the return leg of the tour on the Stevens Canyon and Paradise Valley Roads are prone to avalanche and should be skied with caution. Talk with the ranger at Paradise before starting out.

Access: Drive to the Nisqually Entrance of Mount Rainier National Park, then on to the end of the road at Paradise. The tour starts from the southeast corner of the upper parking lot (5,450 feet).

The Tour: Follow the Paradise Valley Road as it descends below the Paradise Inn and crosses three snow-covered bridges. Directly after the

Cornice on crest of Mazama ridge; Castle and Pinnacle Peaks in distance

third bridge (5,200 feet), turn left and head uphill. If you have climbing skins, this is the time to put them on.

The climb starts out steep but levels out on a small bench. Staying to the right of the creek, ski to the upper end of the bench. At the base of the steep slopes, go right then switchback up to the summit of Mazama Ridge (5,700 feet).

Take time to explore the rolling ridge crest, uninhibited by summer signs that tell you to "Stay on the Trail" and "Keep off the Meadows." Ski over a rolling cushion of snow north toward Panorama Point or to the open basin below Paradise Glacier a little to the east. Excellent campsites abound.

To ski the loop, head down Mazama Ridge, staying to the right of center along the ridge top. Near the southern end of the ridge, the broad plateau falls away. Ski just east of the ridge crest, angling across several open, south-facing slopes and through several bands of trees until you reach the Reflection Lakes Ski Trail. Go left and descend with your best telemark through the heavy timber to Stevens Canyon Road. On the road, ski to the left for 100 feet to reach the first lake at 2½ miles (4,854 feet).

To return, ski west from Reflection Lakes on Stevens Canyon Road. Back at the Reflection Lakes Ski Trail you must make a choice. To continue on the road means crossing a steep avalanche slope above Narada Falls, which is only safe when the snow pack is stable. If following the road, ski about half-way across the avalanche slope, then head uphill on the Paradise Valley Road. If the snow pack is unstable or you simply love the excitement of skiing steep, tree-studded hillsides, then follow the orange stakes marking the trail, up over Mazama Ridge and down to the Paradise Valley Road.

Ski up the Paradise Valley Road through the beautiful snow-covered valley with views of Mount Rainier ahead. The road traverses below Mazama Ridge, passing under an avalanche chute halfway up the valley. Here it is best to ski out into the open valley floor when there is any risk of avalanches.

46 GLACIER VISTA AND CAMP MUIR

Glacier Vista

Class: self-propelled
Rating: backcountry
Round trip: 3 miles
Skiing time: 2 hours
Elevation gain: 1,022 feet
High point: 6,336 feet
Best: December–April
Avalanche potential: low
Map: Green Trails, Mt. Rainier
  East No. 270

Camp Muir

Class: self-propelled
Rating: mountaineer
Round trip: 9 miles
Skiing time: 8 hours
Elevation gain: 4,500 feet
High point: 10,000 feet
Best: mid-October–mid-July
Avalanche potential: moderate
Map: Green Trails, Mt. Rainier
  East No. 270

Though the snow is best from mid-October to mid-July, diehard skiers come here year-round for a few turns. Winter skiers generally are satisfied with the steep slopes at Glacier Vista below Panorama Point. Those continuing to Camp Muir should be proficient mountaineers ready to deal with sudden whiteouts and blasting winds. In summer, skiers must hike to the

Spring skiing on the Muir Snowfield

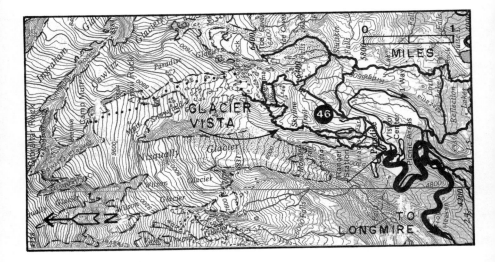

base of the permanent icefield above Pebble Creek (7,500 feet). Even in these milder months be prepared for sudden changes of weather and fogs that erase all landmarks.

Note: When snow conditions are unstable or an east wind is blowing, Panorama Point has high potential for slab avalanches. Stay away after a heavy snowfall, when the wind blows from the east, or during winter rains.

Access: The tour starts from the upper Paradise parking lot (5,450 feet; see Tour 45). At the start and finish of the trip, register in the log book at the ranger's office.

The Tour: Ski up from the parking lot, working your way around the sliding area then climbing along the left side of Alta Vista. Above Alta Vista, follow the flat-topped ridge crest past forlorn clumps of windblown trees to Glacier Vista at 1½ miles (6,336 feet). This overlook of Nisqually Glacier is an ideal picnic spot and turnaround for winter skiers.

To proceed to Camp Muir, climb the southwest rib of Panorama Point through a broken line of dwarf trees. Skis generally are removed in favor of postholing.

Once on top, put the skis back on and head over the rolling summit of Panorama Point, angling to the right until you reach the base of a prominent rock outcrop named McClure Rock. Stay to the left of these rocks and the next rocks, Sugar Loaf, and aim for the next knob, which is Anvil Rock.

Skirt Anvil Rock on the left and ascend the last long snowfield to Camp Muir (10,000 feet). Take special care on the descent. If visibility is poor, stick close to the tracks you made going up. Mistakes in direction on the descent may take you way out of your way, like all the way down to Nisqually Glacier or farther out of your way over a cliff.

 47 COPPER PASS

Class: *groomed*
Rating: *easiest*
Round trip: *5½ miles to pass*
Skiing time: *3 hours*
Elevation gain: *800 feet*

High point: *4,700 feet*
Best: *mid-December–mid-April*
Avalanche potential: *low*
Map: *Green Trails, Mt. Rainier West No. 269*

With all the ski trails within Mount Rainier National Park, it is hard to conceive that a forest road that crosses numerous clearcuts could be one of the most rewarding ski tours in the region. You'll start the tour in the scrub forest of an old clearcut then climb to the ridge tops and views of Mount

Adams, Mount St. Helens, Sawtooth Ridge, High Rock, and the Olympic Range. The real climax of the trip, however, is the magnifying-glass view of Mount Rainier.

This tour is part of the Mt. Tahoma Trails system and is now closed to all motorized use from mid-December to the end of April. The access road to the Sno-Park is plowed on a time-available basis. Do not be surprised if the going is rough when you arrive after a winter storm.

Access: Drive Highway 706 toward the Nisqually Entrance to Mount Rainier National Park for 3.4 miles past the town of Ashford. Turn left on Copper Creek Road No. 59 and follow it for 4.4 miles to the Sno-Park. The road is narrow and steep; *all* vehicles are advised to carry tire chains and a shovel. A side road at the 2.8-mile point offers an alternate starting point when conditions are bad. A Sno-Park permit is required for parking (3,700 feet).

The Tour: Two roads take off from the Sno-Park. Ignore the road on the right, which heads steeply uphill toward Lake Christine. Clip into your binding and begin your tour by striding straight up Road 59. The road climbs gradually, passing a gate and several Mt. Tahoma Trails signs as it heads northwest into a clearcut valley. Before long Mount St. Helens comes into view and ½ mile beyond Mount Adams appears on the horizon. At the end

Mount Rainier from Copper Pass

of the first mile the road divides, with the Champion Trail to Copper Creek Hut (Tour 48) branching off to the left. Stay right and soon after begin a couple of gradual switchbacks; these can be shortcut when ample snows cover the logging debris. At 2¾ miles reach the 4,500-foot Copper Pass at the crest of the ridge and a glorious view of Mount Rainier.

Once you have absorbed the initial impact of this view it is time to check out your options. The road divides at the pass. Road 59, the one you have been following, crosses the ridge. It heads east, descending then climbing to the next ridge before traversing north along the border of the Glacier View Wilderness for 4 miles, offering few views except of the clearcut hills of the Champion Forests.

Your most scenic option from the pass is to take the road to the right.

This road follows the ridge crest south for a mile to the base of Mount Beljica, offering spectacular views for little effort. Near the base of Mount Beljica the road divides; go left for a steep climb to the ultimate viewpoint at 4,860 feet.

If the weather is not good or you are tired of the view (is that possible?), try the 4¾ mile Deer Creek Loop, which heads north from the pass along the clearcut hillsides. The loop descends to 3,660 feet then climbs back to the pass. Along the way you will have to negotiate your skis down the side of a ridge, losing 350 feet of elevation before you regain the road. The route is well marked.

STATE ROUTE 706

48 CHAMPION TRAIL—EAST

Class: *groomed*
Rating: *more difficult*
Round trip: *8 miles*
Skiing time: *4 hours*
Elevation gain: *1,100 feet*

High point: *4,500 feet*
Best: *mid-December–March*
Avalanche potential: *low*
Maps: *USGS, Mt. Wow and Ashford;*
    Green Trails, Mt. Rainier West No. 269

Map on page 134

Beyond a doubt this is the most scenic hut access trail in the entire Mt. Tahoma Trails system. Day skiers, do not ignore this tour simply because you are not planning to spend a night at Copper Creek Hut. This tour has something for everyone: scenery, views, open slopes for telemarking, and miles of roads for exploring.

To spend a night at the hut between December 15 and April 30, you must make an advance reservation. Send a self-addressed stamped envelope to the Mt. Tahoma Trails Association, Attn: Hut Reservation Program, P.O. Box 206, Ashford, WA 98304. Ask for a Hut Reservation Form. Forms are also available at the Bunkhouse in Ashford on Saturdays and Sundays between 9:00 A.M. and 4:00 P.M.

Access: Following the directions given in Tour 47, drive to the 59 Road Sno-Park (3,700 feet).

The Tour: The Sno-Park is located at the intersection of Road 59 and the Lake Christine Trail access road, which is the winter haunt of snow-busting four-wheel-drives. Avoid the motorized jamboree and continue straight on Road 59, skiing past a gate and several signs. The climb is steady but not steep as the road contours around the hillside into the Copper Creek drainage.

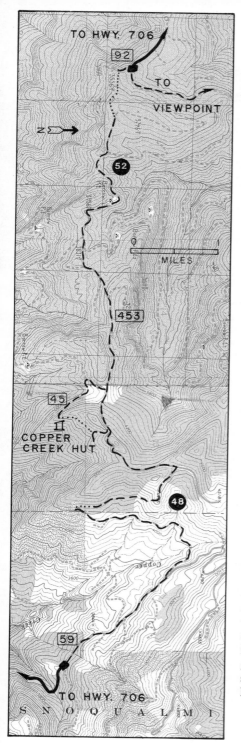

On clear days you will have a magnificent view that includes Mount St. Helens, High Rock, Sawtooth Ridge, and Mount Adams.

At the end of the first mile the road divides (3,900 feet). Go left on a road signed as the Champion Trail and descend gradually to cross Copper Creek. The road then begins a gradual climbing traverse to the southwest across old clearcuts. Mount Rainier soon comes into view and before long dominates the eastern skyline. Ignore all spur roads and continue the easy-going traverse until you reach 2 miles. At this point the road makes a couple of steep climbs then reaches a landing. Here the Champion Trail leaves the road and turns sharply back on itself as you begin a traverse across the hillside. The well-marked trail passes young trees and winds around old stumps for ¼ mile to reach an upper logging platform and another road.

Follow this new road as it climbs to the northeast. This section of the trail offers a chance to enjoy an ever-expanding view of Mount Rainier. The Champion Trail follows the road to the ridge crest then contours around the hill to a saddle and a four-way intersection. At 4,500 feet this is the tour's highest point. Go left on a logging road that descends gradually across a clearcut hillside, crosses an open ridge, then drops to a three-way intersection on a narrow saddle. Copper Creek Hut is now visible on a bench below the road, and you can choose one of two routes to get there. If visibility is good, go left at the saddle and descend a steepish switchback before heading cross-country to the hut.

Mount Rainier from the Champion Trail

When visibility is poor, you should stay on the Champion Trail, which descends very steeply to an intersection on a forested ridge crest at 3 miles. Go left and descend on Road 45 for 500 feet, then take the first left for a final very steep climb to reach 4,200-foot Copper Creek Hut at 3½ miles.

STATE ROUTE 706

49 HIGH ROCK VIEW

Class: *multiple use*
Rating: *easiest*
Round trip: *3–20 miles*
Skiing time: *2–10 hours*
Elevation gain: *up to 2,000 feet*

High point: *up to 4,300 feet*
Best: *January–March*
Avalanche potential: *low*
Map: *Green Trails, Randle No. 301*

Map on page 136

Don't classify this tour as second-rate just because it has no protection from four-wheelers and snowmobilers. Views are outstanding and, when the conditions are right, so is the skiing. To the northeast rises Washington's

View to the north from Road 8415

monarch (Rainier) in her full glory and to the south lie the serrated cliffs of Sawtooth Ridge, which culminate in an obelisk-like spire known as High Rock.

Access: Drive toward Mount Rainier National Park on State Route 706. From Ashford continue east 2.4 miles, then turn left on Forest Road 52 (Karnaham Road). After 1.5 miles, at a four-way intersection, go left onto Skate Creek Road (which is still Forest Road 52). Drive along the valley

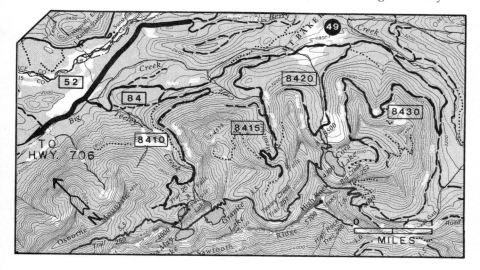

bottom for 3.4 miles, then take a right on Road 84 and drive to the snowline or to one of four spur roads (see below).

The Tours: The first of the four branching roads that make good ski tours starts 1.6 miles from Road 52. Road 8410 leaves Road 84 at 2,320 feet and climbs for 3 miles, gaining 1,600 feet of elevation, up the Teeley Creek drainage. Save this tour for the days when skiing starts at Road 52, as there are few views and frequently little snow on the lower section of the road.

The second road (No. 8415) starts 3 miles from Road 52 and follows Mesatchee Creek for 3 miles. The tour starts at 2,700 feet with views of Nisqually Glacier, winds up through forest to views of High Rock, and ends at the edge of a clearcut (3,700 feet) with views that extend all the way to the Columbian Crest.

The third tour is on Road 8420, starting 4 miles from Road 52 (2,920 feet). The gentle climb parallels Big Creek for 1½ miles to Big Creek Trail (not suitable for skiing) and ends at 2½ miles in a clearcut (3,600 feet). Views along this tour are outstanding, with Mount Rainier dominating the scene and High Rock casting a long shadow over the valley.

The fourth tour starts 6.5 miles from Road 52 and is the best of the bunch. Ski up Road 8430, which starts at 3,300 feet, and climb around a broad hill. Views of Mount Rainier are breathtaking. Near 3½ miles the road divides; go left on Spur Road (8430)042 and ski ½ mile to the end of the road (3,900 feet) in full view of High Rock Lookout. Experienced backcountry skiers may continue on with the help of a map and ski over the next hill to Cora Lake (4,300 feet).

50 SNOW BOWL HUT

Class: groomed
Rating: most difficult
Round trip: 9 miles
Skiing time: 4 hours
Elevation gain: 2,130 feet

High point: 4,350 feet
Best: mid-December–mid-March
Avalanche potential: low
Maps: USGS, Sawtooth Ridge and Anderson Lake

Map on page 139

Snow Bowl Hut lives up to its name. The hut is located at the top of a beautiful, open, north-facing slope where the snow is sheltered from the wind and sun. Few visitors can resist taking at least a couple of runs down the bowl, carving a squiggly track on the soft snow.

Snow Bowl Hut, perched on the crest of the ridge above the bowl, has an

Snow Bowl Hut

outstanding view of Mount Rainier and is a delightful destination for day trips and overnight adventures. Skiers who have managed to remain aloof from the thrills of telemarking will find the hut is an excellent base for explorations into the lesser skied regions of the Mt. Tahoma Trails area.

The hut is open to all on a first-come reservation basis. For a Hut Reservation Form, send a self-addressed, stamped envelope to: Mt. Tahoma Trails Association, Attn: Hut Reservation Program, P.O. Box 206, Ashford, WA 98304.

Access: From the town of Elbe drive Highway 706 east toward the Nisqually Entrance of Mount Rainier National Park. After 7 miles go right on a road signed to the South District Trails. After 1.2 miles this rough, narrow road divides; stay right and cross the Nisqually River. At 3.1 miles you will reach a T intersection, go left. A gate is passed at 5 miles, and at 6.6 miles the plowing ends at the 1 Road Sno-Park (2,240 feet).

The Tour: This tour has a moderately low-elevation start so don't be surprised if you find yourself carrying your skis at the start. Even when snow-covered, the first portion is a challenge; the steep ascent requires a surge of energy from muscles that are stiff from the long drive. If you choose to walk this portion of the tour, please stay to the side of the road. Do *not* leave footprints that could catch the ski of a descending skier.

After climbing steeply for ¼ mile, the road divides. To the right is Anderson Lake (Tour 51). Your road, called the Outer Loop Trail, continues straight, ascending steadily up the forested valley. The climb seems relentless with only two, much too short, level sections where you can stand without

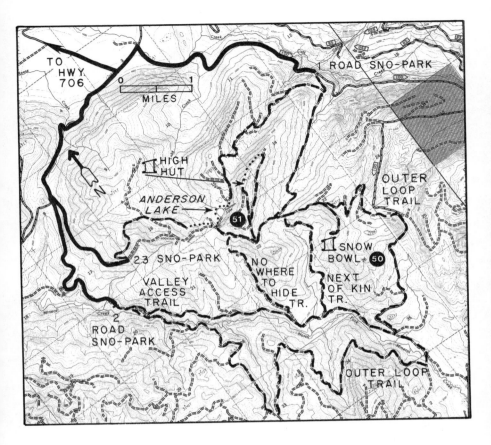

slipping backward. Catt Creek is crossed at 2 miles (3,420 feet), and soon after the road becomes a series of switchbacks.

At 2¾ miles the road reaches the ridge crest and an intersection (3,880 feet). Go left, still on the Outer Loop Trail, and follow a road east along the crest of the ridge.

The road climbs then descends to pass the upper end of the Next of Kin Trail at 3 miles. This intersection marks the end of the grooming. However, that does not mean you must now make your way forward through the unyielding wilderness. This well-used route continues on a road that climbs along the south side of the ridge. Pass a spur road to the right then one to the left before you reach the tour's 4,350-foot high point and views of Snow Bowl and the hut.

From the high point the road descends to an intersection and excellent view of Mount Rainier. Go right, leaving the Outer Loop Trail, and follow the ridge crest for the ½ mile to the hut (4,300 feet).

51 ANDERSON LAKE / HIGH HUT LOOP

Class: self-propelled
Rating: most difficult
Loop trip: 9¼ miles
Skiing time: 6 hours
Elevation gain: 2,603 feet

High point: 4,743 feet
Best: mid-December–mid-March
Avalanche potential: moderate
Maps: USGS, Sawtooth Ridge and
   Anderson Lake

Map on page 139

Skiing to Anderson Lake is certainly not the fastest way to reach High Hut, nor is it the easiest. What this tour offers is fun and variety for the adventurous skier as well as a goodly quantity of incredible views.

This loop is an excellent day tour; however, if you can secure a reservation, treat yourself to an overnight stop at High Hut. The view of Mount Rainier from the hut is awesome, and if you are lucky enough to see a sunset you may want to move in permanently. Reservations are available on a first-come basis from December 15 to the end of April. For a Hut Reservation Form, send a self-addressed, stamped envelope to: Mt. Tahoma Trails Association, Attn: Hut Reservation Program, P.O. Box 206, Ashford, WA 98304.

Access: Drive to the 1 Road Sno-Park (2,240 feet) as described in Tour 50.

The Tour: The loop begins with a very steep ascent from the Sno-Park. After ¼ mile the road divides (2,620 feet). Go right on a road signed to Anderson Lake, leaving the regularly groomed Outer Loop Trail. You will return to this point by the road on the left.

The Anderson Lake route is occasionally groomed and generally easy to follow despite a lack of markers at key intersections. The road heads northwest, climbing steadily around a steep ridge to Bear Basin. Once you have passed around the ridge, your objective is to head up to the top of the ridge above. Along the way you will pass several spur roads. The first branches off to the right shortly after you enter the valley. The next branches to the left. Your road climbs along the creek then crosses it, passing a major spur to the right at about the same time.

As you climb, Mount Rainier comes into view to the northeast, rising above the ridges and gradually dominating the view. Continuing up through the basin, you will pass several minor spurs on the left. The next important intersection is reached as the road approaches the base of the final ridge at the upper end of the basin. Go left here, away from the camel-humped ridge that marks the northwest side of the basin. With a view of High Hut above,

"Roughing it" at High Hut during a blizzard

the road continues with its gradual but steady ascent to reach the 4,150-foot crest of the ridge and upper end of the basin at 2½ miles.

From the ridge crest, stay left following a narrow road on a descending traverse along a steep hillside to the marshy Upper Anderson Lake. The road is located at the base of a cliffy ridge and may be covered with heavy sluffs when the snow is unstable. Use your own judgment here and do not proceed if you are uncertain about the stability of the snow pack.

Ski past the base of the upper lake, then follow the road over a low knoll to a picnic table, usually snow-covered, and a vault toilet. At this point the trail is obscure. Ski straight down the road, pass the toilet, and without changing direction head through a thin band of brush to find a very narrow and very steep trail down to Anderson Lake (3,850 feet). Ski straight across the outlet creek, and stay off the lake. From this point you can follow the well-marked route around the lake and up to the ridge crest, or make your own way to the road at the top (4,130 feet).

Once you are up, ski left to a narrow saddle and intersection, which is reached at the 3½-mile point. Follow the road on the left (southeast) for a nearly level traverse around a clearcut ridge. After ¼ mile you will pass the top of the No Where To Hide Trail, and ¼ mile farther on the High Hut Trail heads up to the left. If time is short you can skip the next 2 miles, the hut, and the best view of the tour. However, if time allows, go left for a mile-long trudge to the top of the ridge. About halfway up you will pass the High Hut Loop Trail; at this point stay left and leave the longer Loop Trail as an option for your return.

Follow the road to the crest of the ridge, then head northeast along the crest for the final climb to the 4,743-foot High Hut. Of all the huts on the Mt. Tahoma Trails system, High Hut has the largest view. Mount Rainier dominates, grandly towering over the hut and filling the northeastern horizon. To the northwest you can see all the way to the Olympics, and at night there is a brilliant glow from the Puget Sound cities. To the east and south, the Goat Rocks, Mount Adams, and Mount St. Helens can be seen over a sea of lesser summits.

If you choose to descend by the High Hut Loop, the route heads northeast from the hut and follows the ridge until intersecting a logging road. The Loop then follows the road back to the High Hut Trail. Descend back to the intersection with the road you followed from the Anderson Lake Trail, then go left for a ½-mile descent to the Outer Loop/Snow Bowl Trail intersection. Go left for a steep 2¾-mile descent down a forested valley to return to the 1 Road Sno-Park and the end of the loop at 9¼ miles.

STATE ROUTE 706

52 CHAMPION TRAIL—WEST / COPPER CREEK HUT

Class: groomed
Rating: more difficult
Round trip: 6 miles
Skiing time: 3 hours
Elevation gain: 900 feet

High point: 4,200 feet
Best: mid-December–mid-March
Avalanche potential: low
Map: USGS, Ashford

Map on page 134

The west end of the Champion Trail is the least demanding of all the hut access routes in the Mt. Tahoma Trails system. Even if your skiing skills are not the greatest, you may sample the joys of skiing into an isolated but comfortable mountain hut. The tour is not only easy—it is a lot of fun with gradual climbs and excellent views over the Nisqually River valley, the Sawtooth Ridge, and Mount Rainier. This is also a delightful tour for day skiers, who can ski to the hut or to the open ridge tops beyond.

Access: From the town of Elbe, drive east on Highway 706 for 6.5 miles, then go left on a narrow road signed for the "92 Road Access," the "Central

Copper Creek Hut

District Access," and the "Elbe Hills ATV" area. The road passes several houses then heads out for a long climb up DNR forest lands. The intersections are well signed and all forks are to the right. After 6.3 steep and rough miles the road arrives at the ridge-top Sno-Park (3,300 feet). *Note:* Do not head up these steep and difficult roads without chains and a shovel in your car.

The Tour: Two tours begin from the Sno-Park. The main road on the left goes northeast for 1¼ miles to a viewpoint. The Champion Trail to Copper Creek Hut is the narrow path on the right. This initial narrow and steep climb is the most difficult section of the tour. Once on the crest of the hill the trail begins an easy contouring ascent to the east.

After ½ mile the Champion Trail joins a wide forest road and descends to the right (east). After two short descents you will begin a gradual but steady climb along the ridge. Routefinding is easy and intersections are well marked. You will pass several minor spur roads on the right and left as well as one major service road that branches right at 1½ miles. Shortly after, the road divides. Stay right on Road 453 and continue to climb.

The Champion Trail heads up and along a broad ridge crest to views of Mount St. Helens and Sawtooth Ridge then steepens for a climb to a forested saddle and the first views of Mount Rainier. The road continues its gradual ascent around the north side of the knoll to reach a second saddle and intersection at 2½ miles. If the hut is your goal, go right and descend on Road 45 for 500 feet then take the first left. This road descends briefly then climbs steeply up an exposed hillside to reach the hut at 3 miles (4,200 feet).

If the hut is not the goal of your tour, continue straight for another ¼ mile on the Champion Trail for a steep and exposed climb to excellent touring on the open ridges above the hut.

53 BEAR MEADOW VIEWPOINT

Class: *multiple use*
Rating: *more difficult*
Round trip: *10 miles*
Skiing time: *4 hours*
Elevation gain: *1,200 feet*

High point: *4,090 feet*
Best: *December–March*
Avalanche potential: *low*
Maps: *Green Trails, McCoy Peak No. 333 and Spirit Lake No. 332*

When covered with a crystalline blanket of snow, Mount St. Helens has a seductive charm and a peacefulness that is reminiscent of its classic, pre-1979 silhouette. A chance for a winter view of this exceptionally beautiful mountain is reason enough for sharing your precious skiing time with

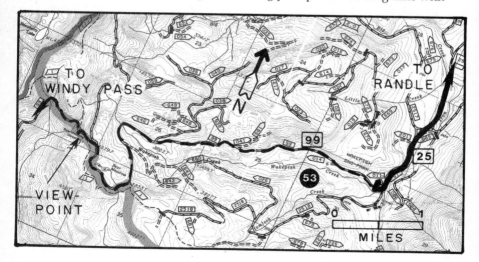

packs of snarling and growling snowmobiles. Of course, if you can schedule your trip for a weekday, you can avoid most of the noisy sleds (snowmobiles).

Access: Drive Highway 12 to Randle, then turn south on the Mount Adams–Cispus Center Road to Mount St. Helens. When the road splits at 0.9 mile stay right on Forest Road 25 and follow it for the next 18 miles to the Road 99 intersection. Go right on Road 99 for 0.1 miles to the Wakepish Sno-Park (2,890 feet). Facilities here include a large three-sided shelter with a wood stove, an information board, and a pit toilet.

The Tour: Before you start out, sign the register at the warming hut and let the Forest Service personnel know that skiers really do have an interest in this area, enjoy the beautiful views, and would return more often if they had a quiet and scenic area of their own.

From the Sno-Park walk back to Road 99 then put on your skis and head up the gated road. After 30 feet of relative calm the snowmobile access trail from the Sno-Park joins in on the right. From this point on the road is rutted and lumpy, somewhat fun to ski when the snow is soft, a bit of a nightmare when it is icy.

The road climbs, never steeply, but with relentless purpose through the forest. Views are few. Initially you will parallel Wakepish Creek, and several cascades can be seen in the narrow gully below the road. Before long the road and creek part company and views are limited to snow- and moss-covered trees and layers of lava seen at the road cuts. At the end of the first mile, Pinto Rock and French Butte come into view over the tree tops to the east.

After the first mile the climb becomes a bit steeper, with just enough grade to ensure an interesting descent. Clearcuts and forested ridges fill the horizon. Spur Road (9900)036 branches right at 3 miles and soon after you will cross Wakepish Creek (3,690 feet). Your road then begins the final long switchback to the saddle at the crest of the ridge.

Skiers near Bear Meadow Viewpoint

Several more spur roads are passed as you climb. To the left an open clearcut invites a couple of telemarks, if the snowmobiles haven't already beaten you to it. The last mile is spent skiing around Bear Meadow, which is hidden in the trees to the right of the road.

At 5 miles the road reaches the saddle. Your destination is the snow-covered viewpoint parking area to the left (4,090 feet). Ski around this open area for the best possible view to the southwest where, weather permitting, you may see the mountain.

You can continue on, leaving the trees for the steep open slopes of the devastation area. Just 5 more miles of skiing will take you to the Road 26 intersection at Meta Lake (3,580 feet). Road 99 ends at the incredible Windy Pass viewpoint, located 16 miles from the Sno-Park. Watch for sluffs and avalanches on the steep hillsides if you go that far.

54 HAMILTON BUTTES

Cat Creek Road

Class: *multiple use*
Rating: *more difficult*
Round trip: *up to 12 miles*
Skiing time: *6 hours*
Elevation gain: *1,800 feet*
High point: *4,400 feet*
Best: *mid-December–March*
Avalanche potential: *moderate*
Map: *Green Trails, Blue Lake No. 334*

Hamilton Buttes

Class: *multiple use*
Rating: *most difficult*
Round trip: *20 miles*
Skiing time: *9 hours*
Elevation gain: *2,878 feet*
High point: *5,478 feet*
Best: *mid-December–March*
Avalanche potential: *moderate*
Map: *Green Trails, Blue Lake No. 334*

On a clear day the view of Mount Adams from Cat Creek Road is worth a lot. It's worth putting up with buzzing snowmobiles, barking dogs pulling sleds, and even churning four-wheel-drives. So is the tour worthwhile on a cloudy day? If you're looking for some great exercise, the answer is yes. And who knows, the clouds may break and give you an unexpected view.

Skiers who are undaunted by the 10-mile road approach will find Hamilton Buttes an exciting destination. Their open slopes challenge skiers to scribe only their best telemarks on the inclined sheet of virgin snow. The buttes are a well-kept secret among backcountry skiers and will probably remain the domain of a chosen few because of the long approach. Skiers who want to fully ski this fantastic playground should plan two days for this trip.

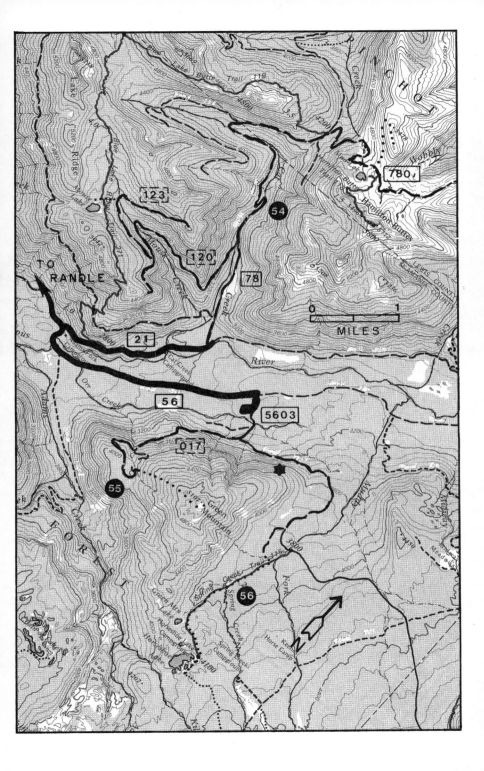

Mount Rainier from the Mouse Creek Road

Access: Drive Highway 12 to Randle then follow combined Forest Roads 23 and 25 south from the center of town. After 0.9 mile the road divides. Stay left on Road 23 and head south 18.7 miles before taking a left on Road 21. Continue on 4.8 miles to an intersection at Adams Fork Campground (2,600 feet). Road 21 is generally not plowed beyond this point during the winter. If the road is open, however, continue on Road 21 for 2 more miles to Cat Creek Road No. 78.

Cat Creek Road: From Adams Fork Campground, ski up Road 21. Except for a climb right after the campground, the way is mostly flat. After 1½ miles, pass Cat Creek Campground and shortly after cross Cat Creek (2,700 feet). The intersection with Cat Creek Road No. 78 is found at 2 miles; ski left here.

Recross Cat Creek at 3¼ miles (3,100 feet), and take a left on Spur Road (7800)120. A steep, rapid climb rounds a shoulder and enters the Mouse Creek drainage. At 5¾ miles cross Mouse Creek, and continue ¼ mile farther to a small logging platform where the whole Cispus River Valley unfolds below your feet east. To the east sits the rounded lump of Potato Hill, and to the south Green Mountain tries unsuccessfully to hide Mount Adams.

Hamilton Buttes: From Adams Fork Campground, ski 2 miles up Road 21, then go left on Cat Creek Road for 5 miles to a pass (4,200 feet). At the far end of the pass, go right on Road 7807, which switchbacks up the clearcut along Timonium Creek.

The base of the buttes is reached at 9 miles, where the road divides. To the right, just over the hill, is little Mud Lake (4,850 feet), a small patch of frozen snow surrounded by ghostly trees, remnants of the fire that swept the buttes bare.

The highest butte, site of an old lookout, is to the south, and located on a cliff—a bit cliffy for good telemarking. If you came to crank turns, head north from the lake to a 5,478-foot butte and pick out the first of many runs from there.

55 GREEN MOUNTAIN

Class: *multiple use*
Rating: *more difficult*
Round trip: *6 miles*
Skiing time: *4 hours*
Elevation gain: *1,000 feet*

High point: *4,000 feet*
Best: *January–March*
Avalanche potential: *low*
Map: *Green Trails, Blue Lake No. 334*

Map on page 147

The Sno-Park system on the north side of Mount Adams was designed for snowmobile use. Radiating from these Sno-Parks are miles of interconnected groomed roads, and the snowmobiles can easily travel 100 miles in a day. With a bit of ingenuity and determination not to be shut out of this beautiful area, skiers can find a few pleasant tours away from the traffic. This tour to Green Mountain is not closed to motors; however, few machines venture onto this short, dead-end road as the miles of groomed roads lure the speed demons elsewhere.

The Green Mountain Road climbs through clearcuts to a tremendous view of Mount Adams—an enjoyable climb and descent for most skiers. Good skiers can reach the backcountry by continuing up from the end of the road to the summit of Green Mountain.

Access: Drive Highway 12 to Randle, then head south on Highway 131, which is also signed to Forest Roads 23 and 25. After 0.9 mile the road divides—stay to the left on Road 23. After 18.7 miles go left again on Road 21. Continue up for the next 4.8 miles to an intersection with Road 56. Go right here on Road 56, passing Adams Fork Campground, which is kept open for self-contained RVs in the winter. Cross the Cispus River then follow the dirt-surfaced Road 56 for another 3.1 miles before turning right on Road 5603

Mount Curtis Gilbert in the Goat Rocks

for a final 0.3 miles to the Orr Creek Sno-Park (2,900 feet). *Note:* The road may not be plowed immediately after every storm. Always carry a shovel and chains for your tires.

The Tour: From the Sno-Park, point your skis up Road 5603, which starts off with a short descent. Once across Orr Creek the road climbs to the base of Green Mountain. Turn right on Road (5603)017 at ¼ mile from the Sno-Park and leave the snowmobile route. Ski southwest, climbing steadily while enjoying views of Juniper and Sunrise Peaks.

At 2¾ miles, round the first switchback into an open clearcut. Ski 500 feet farther until the road levels and then go uphill on an old skid road to reach the ridge top at 3 miles (4,000 feet). Glide, or break trail, west across the old logging platform and look around. On a clear day Mount Adams takes on an overpowering presence to the south, Mount Rainier towers above Cat Creek to the north, and Old Snowy and Gilbert to the east reign over the lesser summits of the Goat Rocks.

Experienced skiers with sights on the summit should stay on Road (5603)017 as it crosses a level bench, passes another clearcut, and then climbs steeply up through the forest. The road deteriorates here. Emerging into an upper clearcut, leave the road and climb straight up. Once in the trees above the clearcut the route is obvious—it follows the ridge line to the summit. You will find this effort is rewarded with views even better than below.

56 HORSESHOE LAKE

Class: multiple use
Rating: backcountry
Round trip: 11¾ miles
Skiing time: 6 hours
Elevation gain: 1,200 feet

High point: 4,100 feet
Best: mid-December–mid-March
Avalanche potential: low
Map: Green Trails, Blue Lake No. 334

Map on page 147

Despite the rough setting in the center of snowmobile country, this tour is a definite gem. The trip begins with a 3-mile ski up a groomed snowmobile road. The constant rip and roar of the machines demands nerves of steel; however, the second half of the tour is on a skier-only trail that tunnels through snow-laden trees, up a forested valley, to Horseshoe Lake.

Overall, this tour is not difficult and, if skiing ability were the only factor, this tour could be given a *more difficult* rating. However, the trail is not well marked and routefinding and map-reading skills are very important. At least one person in the party should have a good sense of direction as well as be competent with map and compass.

Access: Drive to the Orr Creek Sno-Park as described in Tour 55.

The Tour: From the Sno-Park, ski south on Road 5603, which starts off with a short descent to Orr Creek then climbs. At ¼ mile pass Spur Road (5603)017 to Green Mountain (Tour 55). For now you must stay with the snowmobiles and continue up the well-groomed Road 5603. Around the 1-mile point you will pass the only avalanche hazard on this tour as you ski by two narrow chutes where snow spills down from the clearcut hillside above.

After passing the 3-mile mark, continue on to the next corner then go right on a narrow, ungroomed, spur road signed to the Spring Creek Trail. Leave the snowmobiles (hopefully) as you follow the road around the edge of a large clearcut. The road parallels a line of uncut trees for ¼ mile then bends right heading across a plantation of young trees that extends all the way to the base of Green Mountain. As you head out into the plantation, the road disappears in the nearly level field of snow. Look left to the line of trees along the southeast side of the giant plantation, then head for a point about a third of the way to the base of Green Mountain. If there are no other ski tracks to follow, you may have to scout around a bit to find the narrow trail cut, marked with a blue diamond, which heads through the dense grove of trees.

This first section of trail is well marked with blue diamonds. The trail

A snowy day on the trail to Horseshoe Lake

passes through a dense line of trees then skirts a marsh and an old burn. At 4 miles from the Sno-Park, the trail crosses Spring Creek and your reassuring line of blue diamonds comes to an end. Cross the creek, then continue straight ahead with just a single line of trees between you and the marsh, and you should be on the trail.

This skier-only trail is very peaceful as it climbs gradually through the forest. The main noises are the swish of your skis and the thump of your poles. At 4½ miles, pass a signed trail to Keenes Horse Camp. Continue straight and at 5¼ miles you should pass just to the right of the small, forested Green Mountain Lake (4,050 feet).

Continuing through the forest, the climb increases for the final ½ mile. An intersection with the Chain of Lakes Trail marks your arrival at Horseshoe Lake. Follow the trail as it traverses along the left side of the lake to reach the campground at 5¾ miles (4,100 feet). You may find a few snowmobiles around the campground; however, you can avoid them by finding a picnic site away from the campground.

57 PACKWOOD LAKE

Class: *multiple use*
Rating: *backcountry*
Round trip: *9 miles*
Skiing time: *7 hours*
Elevation gain: *500 feet*

High point: *3,200 feet*
Best: *January–April*
Avalanche potential: *low*
Map: *Green Trails, Packwood No. 301*

An example of the difference a blanket of snow can make: Packwood Lake in summer is a turmoil of loud motorcycles and mobs of people trampling shores along the edge of the Goat Rocks Wilderness. In winter it is a silent island of pristine white in a sea of green peace. In summer a 4½-mile trail leads to the lake. In midwinter, if the weather so decides, there may be up to 6 additional miles of road skiing, and you may then have to be contented with just reaching the tour's official starting point at the trailhead parking lot and its broad view over the Cowlitz River Valley to the Tatoosh Range and Mount Rainier. If the lake is the inflexible goal, skiers had best wait until late March or April, when the road is snow-free to the end.

Note: When the snow pack is very stable, snowmobilers and skiers by-pass the trail by following the Pipeline Road/Trail to the lake. At about 2 miles there is a steep side-hill section, prone to avalanches, lasting about ½ mile. If determined to try this approach, which is by far the easier, check

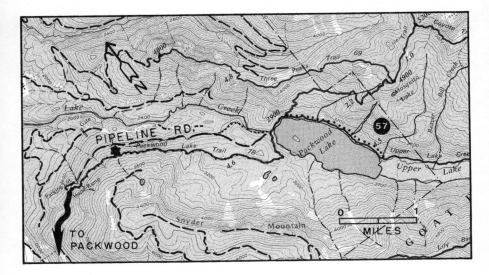

Packwood Lake Trail

with the Packwood Ranger Station, talk to someone who has been over the road recently, or be prepared to turn back if conditions at the slide do not look good. The Pipeline route starts directly below the trail parking lot.

Access: Drive Highway 12 to the Packwood Ranger Station (1,100 feet), then head south for 6 miles (if snow allows) as you follow the Packwood Lake Road to the end (2,700 feet).

The Tour: Starting at the east end of the parking lot, the trail is wide, well graded, and easy to follow over gentle ups and downs. At 3½ miles a window in virgin forest looks north to Rainier. The steepest travel is the final

½ mile, where the trail drops 200 feet to the lake and campsites (2,900 feet).

From the lake the horizon is dominated by huge walls of 7,487-foot Johnson Peak. For a change of scenery, ski the Upper Lake Creek Trail along the east shore, to where Packwood Lake and enclosing forests form a perfect frame for the jolly white giant of the Cascades, Mount Rainier.

When the snow is stable, ski the Pipeline Road, which starts at the base of the parking area. Pass the gate and follow this nearly level road along the side of the steep hill. At 1½ miles the road divides at the slide. Go right on a trail that climbs up and over the worst section. Do not try to cross when the snow pack is unstable or in icy conditions. Near the 3-mile point the road divides again; go straight ahead and parallel Lake Creek to the lake. At 4 miles you must ascend a steep cement ramp up Packwood Dam. Once on top you will intersect the trail just before reaching the lakeshore and campsites.

58 YELLOW JACKET ROAD

Class: self-propelled
Rating: easiest
Round trip: 7 miles
Skiing time: 4 hours
Elevation gain: 480 feet
High point: 4,800 feet
Best: January–March
Avalanche potential: low
Map: Green Trails, White Pass
  No. 303

Map on page 156

There is fun for all in the Yellow Jacket area. The road, nearly level, pleases beginners. Clearcuts challenge telemarkers and telemarker want-to-bes. For everyone there are maximum views for a minimum climb, especially suited to skiers seeking the best in mountain scenery but not really wanting to tackle lofty summits.

"Mother's ski poles are better!"

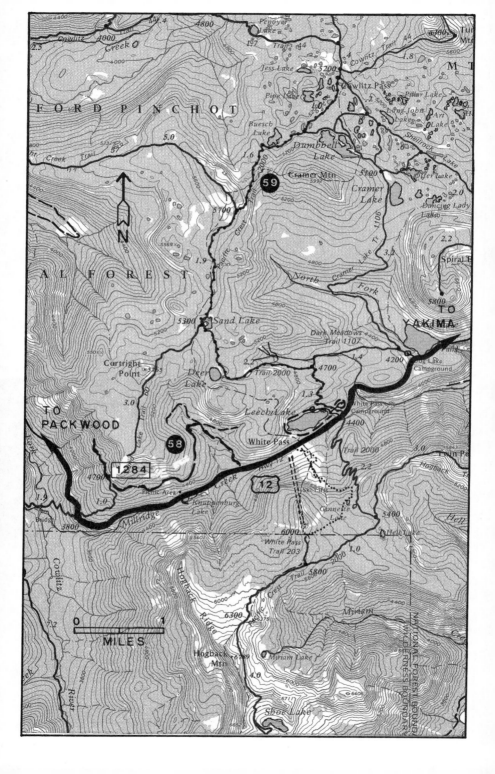

Goat Rocks viewed from Yellow Jacket Road

Access: Drive Highway 12 west for 0.7 mile from White Pass summit, then turn north on Yellow Jacket Road No. 1284. Park well off to the side to allow road-maintenance equipment free access to the work center at the road-end (4,320 feet).

The Tour: The Yellow Jacket Road is a designated cross-country ski area and only a moderate number of snowmobiles get "lost" and end up here. One can follow the tracks of these poor lost souls as they wander around and around in circles.

Elevation is gained gradually along the tree-lined route. At ½ mile is the first clearcut, the best one for showing off downhill turning skills. The road then turns south across open slopes. Southeast, the upper lifts of the White Pass Ski Area come into view. Across the valley massive Hogback Ridge dominates the horizon. The road soon bends west and the Cowlitz River Valley unfolds, a new segment being added with each clearcut traversed. On the horizon there at first is just Chimney Rock, but ultimately views extend deep into the Goat Rocks, all the way to 7,930-foot Old Snowy Mountain. To the north the Tatoosh Range comes into view.

The climax of the trip is at the road-end at 3½ miles (4,800 feet). When the last corner is rounded Mount Rainier emerges in full view, high and mighty above other peaks. Take a long lunch break before heading back to enjoy the miles of vistas.

59 SAND LAKE

Sand Lake

Class: self-propelled
Rating: most difficult
Round trip: 7 miles
Skiing time: 6 hours
Elevation gain: 895 feet
High point: 5,295 feet
Best: January–mid-May
Avalanche potential: none
Map: Green Trails, White Pass
No. 303

Cowlitz Pass

Class: self-propelled
Rating: backcountry
Round trip: 16 miles
Skiing time: 2–3 days
Elevation gain: 1,200 feet in, 500 feet out
High point: 5,600 feet
Best: January–May
Avalanche potential: low
Map: Green Trails, White Pass
No. 303

Map on page 156

Ski to one subalpine lake or to a hundred. Climb to the top of one or many of the countless hills for the sheer pleasure of coming down, or save energy and dignity by contouring forested hillsides to beautiful snow-covered meadows. No matter what kind of cross-country is your cup of tea, the Pacific Crest Trail north of White Pass probably has it. Skiers with only one day may travel to Deer and Sand Lakes. Those with two or more days can ski deep into the lakes area at Cowlitz Pass, a wonderful base camp for explorations in the center of the William O. Douglas Wilderness.

Access: Drive Highway 12 to White Pass summit and park in the over-night parking lot (4,400 feet) near the motel.

The Tour: This tour begins ½ mile below the summit of White Pass. Ski through a narrow band of trees to a prepared cross-country track around Leech Lake. Turn right, paralleling the track to the northeast end of the lake and the Pacific Crest Trail.

The Pacific Crest Trail starts off in forest, switchbacking up a small knoll; the way is usually well tracked and easy to follow as far as Deer Lake. After a new snowfall, however, someone has to be first and it may be you, so be sure to carry a map and compass to navigate over the forested ridges. A brief description: After leaving Leech Lake, when nearing the top of the first hill, head left over a shallow saddle, then contour left around the backside of the open hill above Leech Lake. At 2 miles pass a large meadow on the right. Continue climbing to the left (west) up a steep ridge. A short descent down the opposite side leads to 5,206-foot Deer Lake.

Skiing the Pacific Crest Trail south of Sand Lake

Beyond Deer Lake the trail turns north (right). Head along a broad ridge crest of open forest interspersed with pocket-sized meadows. Sand Lake (5,295 feet) lies ½ mile beyond Deer Lake and is much more difficult to spot—its odd shape makes it look more like a meadow than a body of frozen water. Day skiers will find Sand Lake to be an ideal turnaround point.

The route beyond is a steady climb along the east side of the ridge in view of Spiral Butte (an infant volcano) with occasional looks south to the Goat Rocks and Mount Adams. At 5 miles (5,600 feet), the trail bends right to contour the east side of a partially forested hill and starts a descent that ends 1 mile later at Buesch Lake (5,080 feet). The trail skirts the right side of the lake, then climbs northeast to Cowlitz Pass (5,200 feet) and camping.

Numerous tours can be made from a base camp here. Skilled backcountry skiers may enjoy the ascent of 6,340-foot Tumac Mountain (another potential St. Helens) to excellent views. Other skiers find plenty of room for exploration among the lakes or in Blankenship Meadows on the north side of Tumac.

Continuing north on the Pacific Crest Trail from the lakes looks inviting on the map, but avalanche potential increases dramatically.

60 ROUND MOUNTAIN

Class: self-propelled
Rating: more difficult
Round trip: 9 miles
Skiing time: 5 hours
Elevation gain: 1,280 feet

High point: 4,320
Best: January–March
Avalanche potential: low
Map: Green Trails, White Pass No. 303

Although primarily on a road that tunnels through dense forest, the Round Mountain Tour occasionally yields beautiful, head-on views of the Goat Rocks, where Old Snowy, Ives Peak, and Gilbert Peak, cloaked in their winter whites, dominate the skyline. From road's end, backcountry skiers—capable of reading a map for direction and the slopes for avalanche hazard—will find access to a north-facing bowl just below the summit of Round Mountain. It's a great slope for cranking turns and a superb location for burning film.

Access: Turn south off Highway 12 at 26.2 miles west of the Highway 410 junction or 7.6 miles east of White Pass. Follow Tieton River Road No. 12 for 3.3 miles to the North Fork Tieton River Sno-Park (3,040 feet). Walk or ski ¼ mile back to Round Mountain Road No. (1200)830.

Deep powder on the upper slopes of Round Mountain

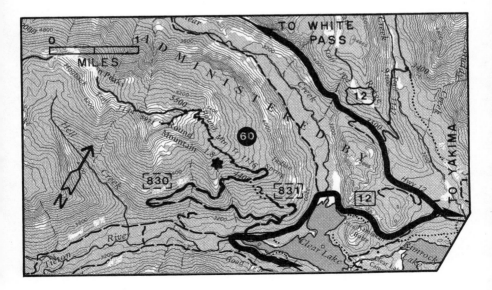

The Tour: The road climbs steadily for ½ mile, passing Road (1200)831, making a switchback, then leveling off at a viewpoint of the Goat Rocks. Visually this is the high point of the tour, although more views of the Goat Rocks, Clear Lake, Pinegrass Ridge, and Russell Ridge await you. For the next 3½ miles, the road alternates between lackadaisical climbing and level traversing. At 4½ miles the road ends at the Round Mountain Trailhead (4,320 feet).

Skiers with *mountaineering* abilities making the summit push or *backcountry* skiers looking for some excitement may shortcut Road (1200)830 by skiing up Road (1200)831, which branches off on the right about ½ mile from the start and provides a more straightforward ascent to the trailhead. Ski to the end of Road (1200)831 then don climbing skins and head to the right, through the trees, to a logging clearing. Ski up the steep clearing to rejoin Road (1200)830, then go right to its end.

At road's end the summit of Round Mountain can be reached by heading up the mountain, sticking to the ridge crest until reaching the edge of the trees at about 5,100 feet. This is a potentially unstable area. When the snow pack is unstable, turn around here and enjoy the run down through the trees. If stable conditions allow, traverse left and climb to the summit ridge. Follow this ridge southwest to the old lookout site (5,971 feet). Before returning, ski off the north side and scribble a signature or two in the tantalizing powder bowl.

61 NORTH FORK TIETON RIVER

Class: *self-propelled*
Rating: *easiest to more difficult*
Round trip: *2–9½ miles*
Skiing time: *up to 5 hours*
Elevation gain: *up to 140 feet*

High point: *3,300 feet*
Best: *January–mid-March*
Avalanche potential: *low*
Map: *Green Trails, White Pass No. 303*

Skiers have five different tours to choose from when they arrive at the North Fork Tieton River Sno-Park. With the exception of the mountaineers' route to the summit of Round Mountain, these tours are all scenic and nonstrenuous, making this an ideal touring area for your entire extended family.

For details of the Round Mountain trip see Tour 60. The remaining four tours are described below.

Access: From the junction of Highway 12 and Highway 410, drive west on Highway 12 for 26.2 miles to the Tieton River Road. (From the west side of the Cascades this intersection is located 7.6 miles east of White Pass.) Follow the Tieton River Road south for 3.3 miles to the North Fork Tieton River Bridge and Sno-Park (3,040 feet).

West Loop: This is a 2-mile tour with a *more difficult* rating. The tour starts from the upper end of the Sno-Park and heads uphill into the trees. Part of the loop is spent traversing open clearcuts with views of the towering walls of the valley. The most challenging portion of the loop is a run through the trees on a narrow trail. At the end of the first mile, the loop route descends to intersect Forest Road 1207. Go left and complete your loop with an easy 1-mile road ski back to the Sno-Park.

East Loop: Varied scenery is the attraction of this *easy* 2-mile loop. From the Sno-Park walk a few feet back down the Tieton River Road to find a blue diamond on the left where the loop begins. The trail passes through forest and clearcuts at the base of Round Mountain, paralleling the road north for a mile. You then must walk, or ski, across the road to find the return leg of the loop that runs along the shores of Clear Lake for a mile.

Third Loop: This 2-mile loop has one short, steep descent, which accounts for its *more difficult* rating. From the Sno-Park walk across the North Fork Tieton River Bridge then on up the road for 200 feet until you find a forest road on the right. Ski uphill to a three-way intersection and go left for a gradual ascent. At the time of this writing many of the blue diamonds that mark this route were missing, including the one that should mark the next intersection. At ¾ mile you must go left on a narrow spur road that descends through a clearcut. At the base of the clearcut, make a short traverse then descend down to the road.

On the pavement, walk a few feet to the right to find snow-covered road and ski down into a camparea. Follow the road until you find a blue

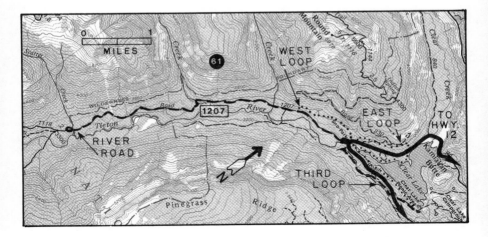

North Fork Tieton River Road

diamond on the left, then ski the marked trail back along Clear Lake to the North Fork Tieton River Bridge.

North Fork Tieton River Road: This is the *easiest* of the five tours that start from the Sno-Park. Snow lingers on this road long after it has disappeared from the three loop routes.

The directions for this tour are delightfully simple. From the upper end of the Sno-Park, follow Road 1207 southeast along the valley floor through forest and clearcuts. Near the 1-mile point pass the West Loop intersection. At 1¼ miles the road descends to cross Hell Creek then climbs in a gradual fashion to cross Miriam Creek at 2½ miles. Do not turn around until you have seen the view of Bear Creek Mountain, Devils Horns, Tieton Peak, and the Goat Rocks from a bend in the road at 2¾ miles.

The road ends at 4¾ miles at the boundary of the Goat Rocks Wilderness. A small campground and a trailhead mark the turnaround point.

62 LOST LAKE

Class: *multiple use*
Rating: *more difficult*
Round trip: *10 miles*
Skiing time: *6 hours–2 days*
Elevation gain: *1,250 feet*

High point: *3,800 feet*
Best: *January–March*
Avalanche potential: *none*
Map: *Green Trails, Rimrock No. 304*

Have no fear, Lost Lake is lost no more. In summer a paved road winds up from the valley floor to a small lakeside campground nestled below the fortresslike summits of Divide Ridge. In winter the road becomes a snow-covered avenue through parklike forests of ponderosa pine. A camp at Lost Lake is ideally situated for exploring the many roads and trails that criss-cross the area's meadows and lakes. Do carry a map and a compass here, in case you get lost among the maze of roads and snow-covered trails.

Access: Drive Highway 12 east from White Pass 16.4 miles (or 0.6 mile west of Hause Creek Campground). Turn south on Tieton Road and drive 0.2 mile to a large Sno-Park on the right (2,550 feet). Here a large Forest Service information sign marks the start of the Goose Egg Trail, a fun 4-mile ski through the forest for novices. If there is ample snow to ski, park here. If

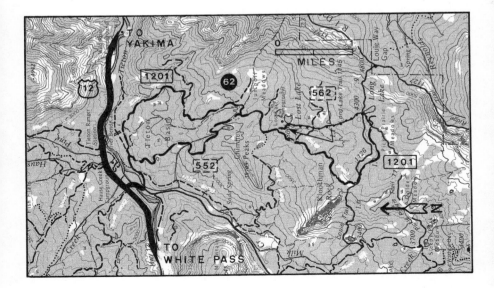

Lost Lake and Divide Ridge

not, turn left on Lost Lake Road No. 1201 and continue driving to the snowline.

The Tour: Elevation is gradually gained on the first mile of the Lost Lake Road. Several spur roads are passed—three on the right and two on the left— then the uphill grade increases slightly. Few views adorn the road but the white snow, green pine needles, orange-red bark of the ponderosa, and blue sky more than compensate. After 2½ miles, snow-plastered Bethel Ridge highlights the northern horizon. At 4¾ miles go left on Spur Road (1201)562 for the final ¼-mile push to Lost Lake and the campground (3,800 feet).

Those of you who would like to get thrown for a loop can now ski Long Lake Trail No. 1145 from the west end of Lost Lake. The mile-long trail winds through forest, crosses logging roads, and cuts through clearcuts. Because the trail is rarely visible under a heavy blanket of snow, expect to navigate with your map and compass.

At Long Lake ski right (west) past a small shelter, and follow the road out to a large parking lot. Turn left here and ski ⅛ mile to Road 1201. (Pickle Prairie Meadows off to the left offer more fine skiing.) To close the loop, ski to the right, down Road 1201 for 3 miles back to the Lost Lake turnoff.

For a looping return to the start, at ¾ mile below Lost Lake go left on Road (1201)552. You will rejoin Road 1201 just ½ mile from the Sno-Park.

63 BEAR CANYON

Class: *multiple use*
Rating: *more difficult*
Round trip: *10 miles*
Skiing time: *4 hours*
Elevation gain: *2,200 feet*

High point: *4,200 feet*
Best: *January–February*
Avalanche potential: *high*
Map: *Green Trails, Tieton No. 305*

Visit Bear Canyon to explore—not to speed through. This narrow cleft twisting through the steep hillsides is characterized by beautiful red cliffs of columnar basalt. Some of the cliffs lie tinseled with giant icicles while the surrounding trees are flaked with snow. And usually the tracks of coyote and elk weave irregular patterns across the white blanket over which you ski.

A word of warning about skiing this scenic, narrow canyon: Avoid it on very warm days, during or after heavy snowfall, or during unseasonal rains. At such times high avalanche danger exists.

Access: Drive Highway 12 east from White Pass 20.5 miles or west from the Highway 410 turnoff for 4.7 miles, turn north onto Bear Canyon Road and park (2,000 feet).

The Tour: Start with an easy ski across the open flood plains of the Tieton River Valley. Follow the road to a narrow cliff in the solid line of

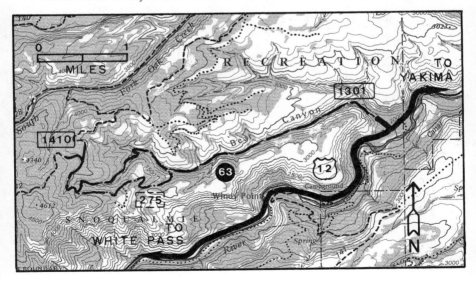

Frozen waterfall in Bear Canyon

the valley walls and skim below the base of a tall wall of columnar basalt.

Once under the cliffs, Bear Canyon Road temporarily ends. The valley narrows here and Bear Creek frequently floods the entire area. Ski left of the road and, for the next ¼ mile, cross and recross the creek several times following the path of least resistance up the valley. Bear with it; the washout eliminates four-wheel-drives and snowmobiles at this end of the valley.

Beyond the washout, follow a section of road littered with boulders. Thread through these obstacles and some brush until the road and valley open up to longer stretches of free skiing.

At 3 miles, after crossing Bear Creek some fourteen times, come to Spur Road (1301)275, which takes off to the left. If you feel like leaving the valley floor for a view, ski up this steep spur road to the first corner and a delightful lunch spot. Spur Road (1301)275 may be followed up and over a 4,000-foot hill to rejoin Bear Canyon Road in 1½ miles.

Continuing up the valley on Bear Canyon Road, you will notice increasing evidence of the snowmobiles that reach this area from Oak Creek. The road begins to climb, giving the promise of a delightful descent and views of the endless procession of snow-covered hills confining the valley.

At 4½ miles Road (1301)275 rejoins Bear Canyon Road (3,800 feet). The road then makes a quick switchback, marking the final push out of the canyon to the ridge top. Now a short descent leads to the upper end of Road 1410 from South Fork Oak Creek (4,000 feet). The world is spread out before your skis. Glistening meadows and open forest beckon you to explore farther—just remember it gets dark early in the canyon, so allow plenty of time for the return trip.

64 THE ELK TOUR

Class: *multiple use*
Rating: *more difficult*
Round trip: *4 miles or more*
Skiing time: *2 hours or more*
Elevation gain: *1,100 feet or more*

High point: *3,600 feet and up*
Best: *January–February*
Avalanche potential: *low*
Maps: *Green Trails, Tieton No. 305 and Manastash Lake No. 273*

Map on page 170

It's like being on safari. You'll see the hoofprints, the tufts of hair, and the ever-present droppings. You'll also see the mighty elk themselves, so come armed with a camera, and the trophies from your safari may be some beautiful pictures for your wall.

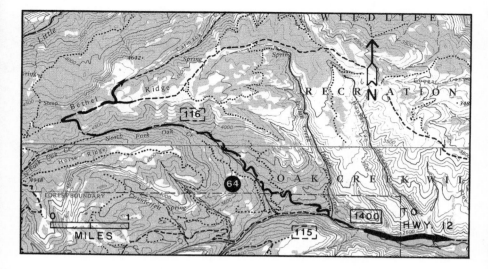

This tour visits the Oak Creek Wildlife Area, an elk feeding station set up to keep hungry animals out of the farms and orchards down the valley and to keep them out of the farmers' stewpots. The elk are fed daily at specific locations and the public is welcome to watch. January is the best time to see the animals; winter is at its peak and the elk rely on the feeding for survival. By February, portions of the herd have wandered away to fend for themselves, and skiers will find elk trails winding up and over the mountains.

Access: Drive Highway 12 west 1.2 miles from the Highway 410 junction (or east 32.6 miles from White Pass). Oak Creek Road is located on the north side of Highway 12 and is open to the public from 9:00 A.M. to 4:00 P.M. Try to arrive by 9:00 A.M. to watch the elk feeding, 3 miles from the highway. Skiing starts 4 miles from the main highway (2,500 feet).

The Tour: Frankly, the first section of the tour is unpleasant. You start out on a road shared with a crew of snowmobiles, four-wheel-drives, and cars that think they are four-wheel-drives. This lasts for ½ mile to the first intersection. Go uphill on Road (1400)115, signed "North Fork Oak Creek," and after 200 feet take a left turn onto Road (1400)116, leaving behind all but the skiers and the snowmobiles.

Climb steadily through forest and past several open areas, paralleling the elk pathways. You will probably see a lot of coyote tracks following the elk's. At 1½ miles (3,100 feet) comes an opportunity to leave behind the snowmobiles. There's no mistaking this intersection, as it's the first one in a mile. This road climbs to the right, heading steeply up for ½ mile, then dies out at 3,600 feet.

Elk sparring near feeding area

Skiers choosing to ski farther should stay with Road (1400)116 and climb along North Fork Oak Creek. The road splits at 5 miles; the left fork stays with the creek and the right fork climbs up to join the Bethel Ridge Road at 5¾ miles.

No matter how great the snow or how blue the sky, don't forget that the gate is locked at 4:00 P.M.

65 PLEASANT VALLEY LOOP

Class: *self-propelled*
Rating: *easiest to most difficult*
Round trip: *up to 14 miles*
Skiing time: *up to 8 hours*
Elevation gain: *10–400 feet*

High point: *3,600 feet*
Best: *January–mid-March*
Avalanche potential: *none*
Map: *Green Trails, Bumping Lake No. 271*

Sandwiched between steep walls of Fifes Ridge and American Ridge, the snow lingers in Pleasant Valley long after it has melted on the surrounding ridges. Fourteen miles of looping trails have been developed by the Cascadians of Yakima, allowing skiers of all abilities to take advantage of the snow.

The Pleasant Valley area is forested and best skied after a fresh snowfall. Icy trails, difficult creek crossings, and deep tree wells are persistent hazards when skiing on old snow.

The Pleasant Valley Loop divides into two subloops, and there is a third loop that has been designed with the needs of beginning skiers in mind.

Access: From the intersection of Highways 410 and 12, drive toward Chinook Pass on 410 to reach the first of four Sno-Parks at 33.3 miles. The first Sno-Park is at Hells Crossing Campground (3,280 feet). Alternate starting points are located at the Crow Lake Way Trailhead, Pleasant Valley

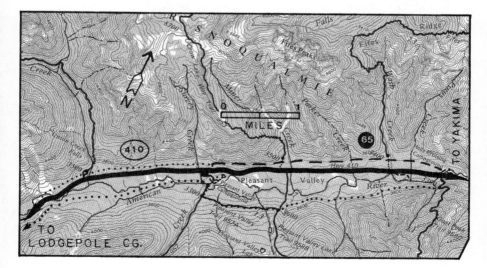

Bridge over the American River at Pleasant Valley Campground

Campground, and the Union Creek Trailhead. Limited parking may also be found at Lodgepole Campground. Be sure to carry chains and shovel at all times on this road; it is plowed on a low-priority basis.

The Beginners Loop: This loop is approximately 2 miles long and is rated as *easiest*. The loop is on old road and is definitely pleasant.

Pleasant Valley Loop—East Half: This 8-mile section runs from Hells Crossing Campground to Pleasant Valley Campground and back. The two legs of the loop, on opposite sides of the American River, differ radically. The southeast leg follows a narrow trail along a rolling hillside and is rated *most difficult*. The northwest side follows a skid road that is wide, open, and nearly level the whole distance—good skiing for everyone. The only point of possible confusion on this loop is the unsigned three-way intersection across the American River from Pleasant Valley Campground. This intersection should not cause problems if you keep on the look-out for it, ski straight through it, and do not wander off following the wrong line of blue diamonds.

Pleasant Valley Loop—West Half: The west half of the loop is a challenging 6 miles of trail skiing from Pleasant Valley Campground to the American River Bridge and back. Both legs on this portion of the loop are rated as *most difficult* and skiers must be ready for several short, steep sections in the trees. At the upper end of the loop you must walk the road bridge across the American River then climb the steep snow bank along the left edge of the road to find the trail on the opposite side.

On the southwest side of the American River, the trail divides. The loop route goes left, heading northeast, back down the river to Pleasant Valley Campground, while the trail on the right makes a challenging roller-coaster run along Highway 410 to Lodgepole Campground. At Pleasant Valley Campground you must also be alert for an unsigned intersection. Here one trail heads north toward the campground while the second trail continues down-valley to Hells Crossing.

66 ALMOST A LOOP OF BUMPING LAKE

Class: multiple use
Rating: easiest
Round trip: up to 12 miles
Skiing time: 1–6 hours
Elevation gain: none

High point: 3,460 feet
Best: January–February
Avalanche potential: low
Map: Green Trails, Bumping Lake
No. 271

Camp robbers are not shy.

In the early 1980s Bumping Lake Reservoir was overrun by snowmobiles who scared skiers away to more congenial areas. But in 1984, the creation of the William O. Douglas Wilderness closed the hills on the east and west sides of the lake to all forms of motors. While the lake and adjacent logging roads remain open, snowmobiles are no longer free to roam the ridge tops and no longer swarm to this area like an invasion of the Chinese army. Don't feel too sorry for the gas guzzlers, as they still have all of the Little Naches as well as the Naches River area for their playground. Meanwhile, skiers are slowly rediscovering Bumping Lake.

The reservoir's low winter water levels expose a broad, open shore between the lake and forest that is ideal for skiing. You'll find long level sections for gliding, short descents for practice turning, and delightful views of the surrounding wilderness.

In theory, it is possible to ski all the way around the lake on the shore area. In reality, two obstacles interfere: the Bumping River at the southwest end of the lake and a steep hill on the southeast side. So instead of one long loop, we suggest you try two shorter loops.

Access: Drive the Bumping River Road to its end (3,460 feet; for directions see Tour 67).

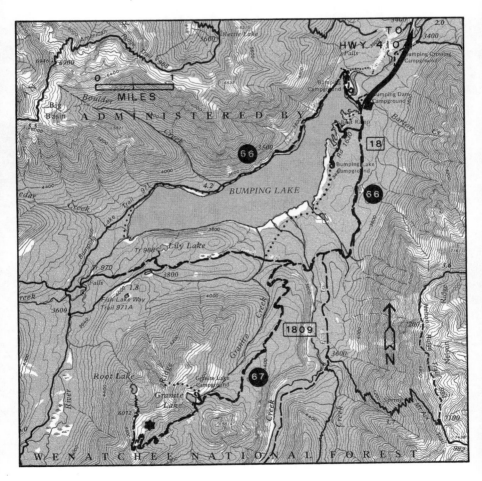

Snow-covered tree stumps at Bumping Lake Reservoir

The Tour: For the first loop, ski north across the dam from the parking area. On the far side, follow the summer road to the left through trees for 1½ miles. Pass the marina and a group of summer cottages. When the road ends, ski down to the shore on the lake trail. Go left and ski back to the dam along open shore, playing slalom between the snow-crested stumps. Avoid skiing on the lake. No matter how solid it may appear, thin spots in the ice are common, especially near the dam. For those wishing to go farther, ski the shoreline for 3 miles from the road's end to the Bumping River at the far end of the lake.

The second loop starts from the parking area and follows Forest Road 18 on the east side of the lake. At ¼ mile ski to the right on the Boat Ramp Road and descend gently toward the shore. Near the lake turn left and ski ½ mile to Bumping Lake Campground. Cruise around the campground loop, then descend to the open shoreline and ski back to the dam and parking area along the edge of the lake.

67 MINERS RIDGE

Class: *multiple use*
Rating: *more difficult*
Round trip: *17 miles*
Skiing time: *8 hours*
Elevation gain: *2,612 feet*

High point: *6,072 feet*
Best: *mid-December–April*
Avalanche potential: *moderate*
Map: *Green Trails, Bumping Lake No. 271*

Map on page 175

Miners Ridge almost has a view. There is almost a view of Mount Rainier, almost a view of Bumping Lake, almost a view of American Ridge, and almost a view of Nelson Ridge. But a thin veil of trees always seems to be in the way. Not until you've gone the full 8 miles and reached the summit of Miners Ridge are you rewarded with a full panoramic display of peaks.

Access: Drive Highway 12 to the Highway 410 turnoff and head up the Naches River Valley and then the American River Valley for 28.5 miles. Turn left at the Bumping River Road turnoff and drive to the parking area (usually another 11 miles) at the end of the plowed road (3,460 feet).

The Tour: Start by skiing up the east side of Bumping Lake on Forest Road 18, admiring the towering summits of Nelson Ridge, almost visible through the trees. This first section of the tour is fairly level and the miles tick off rapidly on a road smoothed by frequent snowmobile use.

The first major intersection occurs at 2½ miles; go right, still on Road 18. At 3 miles comes a second junction (3,580 feet). Turn left on Miners Ridge Road No. 1809 and shed a layer of clothing in anticipation of the work to come. The climb becomes steady and the road makes several switchbacks before easing off on the broad crest of a densely forested ridge. Take time during the climb to enjoy the almost-view of Mount Rainier and to study the snow-measuring equipment on the left side of the road.

Just when it appears the road will dead-end into a steep hillside, the route swings west, following a climbing traverse up to Granite Lake and a campground at 6½ miles (5,060 feet). The lake and campground offer an enjoyable place to camp. They also mark the turnoff for those who would prefer skiing untracked slopes to the ridge top. The route is simple: stay to the northeast end of the lake and follow the trees to the top of the ridge.

Beyond the lake the road climbs to a small pass, then takes a nearly level, mile-long traverse south, entering into a zone of potential avalanche hazard along some steep, exposed sections.

At about 7½ miles the traverse ends and the road starts a determined

Skiing the untracked slopes

climb toward the top. Finally you emerge from the trees to those satisfying views (5,680 feet). The road goes over the top of the ridge and heads down the other side ⅛ mile, but the best views lie along the ridge crest.

68 MOUNT ADAMS

Class: *self-propelled*
Rating: *mountaineer*
Round trip: *8 miles*
Skiing time: *10 hours*
Elevation gain: *6,000 feet*

High point: *12,276 feet*
Best: *May–mid-July*
Avalanche potential: *low*
Maps: *USGS, Mount Adams West and*
Mount Adams East

We all have favorite ski tours—ones we can't find enough superlatives to describe—and in our opinion the tour up the long southern ridge of Mount Adams qualifies as one of the finest trips in Washington.

The trek up the state's second highest peak roughly follows the old mule trail to the summit and is entirely crevasse-free. Views of the surrounding volcanoes—Hood, St. Helens, Rainier—reward your toil, but the real prize

178

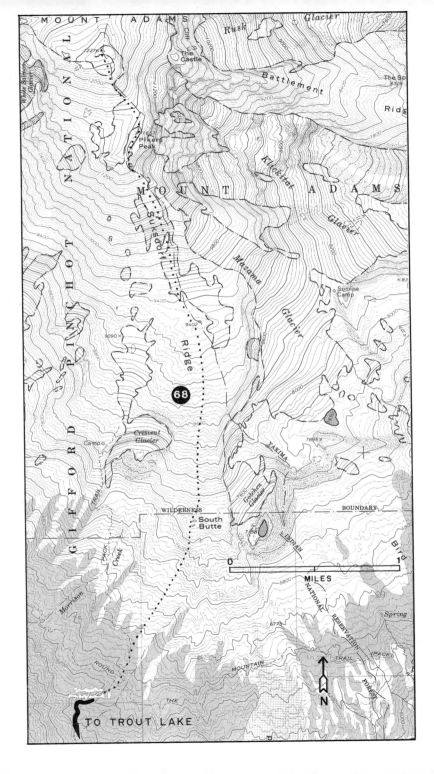

MOUNT ADAMS

MOUNT ADAMS NATIONAL

GIFFORD PINCHOT NATIONAL

Rush Glacier

The Castle

Pikers Peak

Mount Suksdorf

Cliff

The Sp

Battlement

Ridg

Klickitat Glacier

Mazama Glacier

Ridge

9402

68

Sunrise Camp

×83

Crescent Glacier

Camp

YAKIMA

Crofsen Glaciers

7895×

7600

WILDERNESS   BOUNDARY

South Butte

PACK Creek

Morrison

ROUND

Mountain

THE

0   1

MILES

Indian

NATIONAL

RESERVATION

TRAIL (PACK)

Bird

Spring

6773

FOREST

N

TO TROUT LAKE

The old lookout at the summit of Mount Adams is visible in late summer only.

is the descent. Imagine a 6,000-foot vertical drop down a 4-mile ridge and you'll understand why people come back year after year.

Although the skiing is not difficult, this tour is extremely demanding. Skiers must carry the survival gear necessary for climbing any major peak. Prepare yourself for sudden changes in the weather; carry wands and a compass to aid in the descent should clouds quickly engulf the summit, as they are known to do.

The long south-facing slope is often ready for skiing before the access roads are snow-free. Call the Ranger Station at Trout Lake for road conditions before establishing a date to ski the mountain. In May, plan on an overnight tour that could include up to 7½ miles of road skiing to reach Timberline Camp. In mid-July plan on having to walk as much as a mile from the end of the road to reach snow.

Access: Early-season access to Mount Adams is via Columbia River Highway 14 and State Route 141 to Trout Lake, where climbers and skiers must register at the Ranger Station. Then head 1.4 miles north of Trout Lake on Highway 141. When the road divides, go right on a road signed "Mount Adams Recreation Area" and drive 0.6 mile before turning left on Road 80.

Follow signs to Morrison Creek Campground, then on to Timberline Camp at road's end (6,000 feet). Road numbers change during the drive from 80 to 8040 then to Spur Road 500.

Later in the season, skiers coming from the north can save considerable time by driving Forest Road 23 south from Randle to Trout Lake.

The Tour: Leave Timberline Camp from the west side of the climbers' parking area, following a low ridge north and slightly east. Angle around the west side of South Butte to the base of Suksdorf Ridge (7,600 feet). Using the right side of the ridge as a guide, follow it to the false summit (11,657 feet).

Ski over the level crater then up the final, rather steep 600 feet to the true summit (12,276 feet). Weather and time permitting, plan a long rest at the summit—your thighs are going to need help to survive that long run down. On clear days look down on Mount Jefferson, Mount Hood, Goat Rocks, and Mount St. Helens. Then turn north and look up to Mount Rainier—the only point in Washington State that stands over you.

On the descent, stay close to your ascent route. Avoid the tendency to drift east onto the open and crevassed slopes of Mazama Glacier or west into avalanche-prone gullies.

TROUT LAKE

69 BIG TREE LOOP

Class: groomed
Rating: easiest
Loop trip: 4.8 miles
Skiing time: 3 hours
Elevation gain: 400 feet

High point: 2,850 feet
Best: January–February
Avalanche potential: none
Map: Green Trails, Mt. Adams West No. 366

Map on page 182

Loop through majestic pine and fir forest to the base of the largest known ponderosa pine tree, the Trout Lake Big Tree, on this very easy road loop. Weather permitting you will also be treated to a stunning view of Mount Adams.

Access: Follow Highway 14 along the Columbia Gorge to Bingen, then head north on Highway 141 for 23 miles to Trout Lake. When the road divides at the Trout Lake Service Station (a Chevron Station in 1994), stay to the right, and to the right at all the subsequent major intersections. At 4.8 miles from Trout Lake the county road becomes Forest Road 82 and the

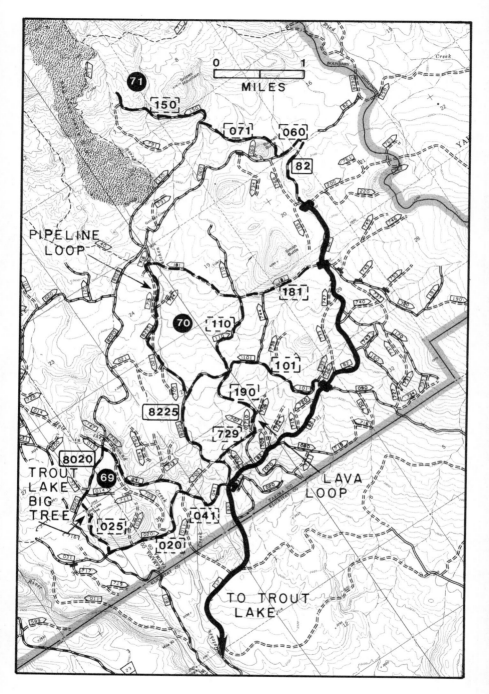

71

150

071   060

82

PIPELINE
LOOP

181

70   110

101

8225   190

729

8020   LAVA
TROUT   LOOP
LAKE   69
BIG
TREE   041

025   020

TO TROUT
LAKE

Sign at the base of Trout Lake Big Tree

pavement ends. At this point you will find the entrance to the Pine Side Sno-Park on your right (2,750 feet).

The Tour: From the Sno-Park walk back across Road 82 to find two cross-country ski trailheads. Head out on the lower of the two trails, which begins with a gradual descent on Spur Road (8200)041. The road is lined with tall pines that create a majestic corridor under a cover of fresh snow.

At the end of the first ½ mile you will reach an intersection that marks the start of the loop portion of the tour (2,650 feet). Stay to the left and continue your journey beneath the towering trees. Wildlife abounds in this area; watch for snowshoe hares or squirrels prancing over the snow. In late winter larger animals such as deer and elk are often spotted.

The next junction is reached at 1½ miles (2,580 feet). Go right here on Spur Road (8000)025 following a trail of blue diamonds. The road is now so narrow you may feel you are really heading out through the wilderness.

At the 2-mile point the tour reaches the Trout Lake Big Tree. A picnic table located near the base of this 200-foot tall tree is an excellent location for lunch as well as for peaceful reflection of nature's wonders.

From the Trout Lake Big Tree, ski past the information board and head straight (north) to Road 8020. Go right on this major forest road, which ascends gradually for the next ½ mile to a clearcut where Mount Adams dominates the northern skyline.

At 3 miles you will turn right on Road (8200)041 and begin a gradual descent that lasts for a mile. The loop is closed at 4 miles and the final ½ mile is spent following your tracks back to the Sno-Park.

70 PINE SIDE LOOPS

Class: *groomed*
Rating: *more difficult*
Loop trip: *7 miles*
Skiing time: *3 hours*
Elevation gain: *930 feet*
High point: *3,680 feet*
Best: *January–February*
Avalanche potential: *none*
Map: *USFS, Mt. Adams Ranger District*

Map on page 182

The perfect sylvan scene, where snow-covered trees line the route as you pass from one forest glade to the next. The only noise you will hear comes from high-spirited skiers as they swoosh down a hill. Okay, the glades are actually clearcuts and your route is a logging road; however, the Pine Side Loops are still a delightful place for a half-day tour by yourself or with your whole family.

"Faster Dad, go faster!"

The loops originating from the Pine Side Sno-Park are groomed and tracked for skiers; perfect for the classic kick and glide style of skiing. Skaters may use the center lane, although it is a bit narrow if you have a wide stride.

Access: Drive Highway 14 along the Columbia Gorge to Bingen then head north on Highway 141 for 23 miles to Trout Lake. When the road divides at the Trout Lake Service Station, stay right. After 1.4 miles the road divides again—stay right. Beyond this point the intersections are all well marked. At 2.1 miles the road divides again—stay right. The county road becomes Forest Road 82 and at 4.8 miles the pavement ends. At this point a right turn will take you into the entrance of the Pine Side Sno-Park (2,750 feet).

The Pine Side Sno-Park is the first and largest of three accesses to the loops. The second access is located 1.8 miles farther up Road 82 at the Road (8200)101 intersection and has parking for four to eight vehicles. If you choose to start your tour here, add an extra mile to the overall mileage.

The third access is located 3.6 miles above the Pine Side Sno-Park at the

Crossing a clearcut on the Lava Loop

Road (8200)181 intersection (3,737 feet) and is also very limited in parking space. If you start your loops here you will end the day with a ½-mile climb back to your car.

Note: The road to the Sno-Park is generally plowed only once a week. Always carry a shovel and tire chains for your car.

The Tour: This tour description starts from the Pine Side Sno-Park. Trail maps, which help you locate the other Sno-Parks, are available at the Mount Adams Ranger Station in Trout Lake. All access points are well marked and all trails and intersections are signed.

From the Pine Side Sno-Park walk across Road 82 then head up Road 8225 following signs for the Lava Loop. The road climbs for ½ mile to an intersection and the start of the Lava Loop. Go right and ski beneath a band of trees before beginning your climb through a series of logging clearings. An intersection marks the top of the loop at 2¼ miles from the Sno-Park. At this point you may either go left and return to the Sno-Park or take a right and continue on to the Pipeline Loop.

Pipeline Loop begins 500 feet above the top of the Lava Loop. At this intersection you should base your choice of direction on snow condition and your skiing ability. If you choose to go left, you will have a gradual climb and an exciting descent. If you go to the right, you will have the steeper climb on the way up and a gradual descent on the way back.

No matter which way you go, at 3¾ miles from the start you will reach the top of Pipeline Loop (3,680 feet). Descend back to Lava Loop, then stay right for the final descent back to the Sno-Park. Watch for elk as you descend. Even if you do not see the animals you may find their deep tracks crossing the road near the clearcuts.

71 GOTCHEN CREEK

Class: *self-propelled*
Rating: *more difficult*
Round trip: *6½ miles*
Skiing time: *3 hours*
Elevation gain: *668 feet*

Map on page 182

High point: *4,520 feet*
Best: *mid-December–March*
Avalanche potential: *low*
Map: *USFS, Mt. Adams Ranger District*

A high plateau at the base of Mount Adams offers excellent skiing and a closeup view of the mountain. The plateau is crisscrossed with a maze of logging roads for skiers to explore while the huge, wide clearcuts are an invitation for family fun. Towering over all, the ice-covered mass of Mount Adams creates a stunning background.

The tour to Gotchen Creek follows a series of mostly level logging roads. The only climbing comes in the final mile as you approach the creek area. Qualified *backcountry* skiers can continue on from the end of the road and head up to the ridge crests for some telemarking descents.

Access: From Highway 14 in the Columbia Gorge, turn north at Bingen and follow Highway 141 for 25 miles to the town of Trout Lake. When the road divides at the Trout Lake Service Station, stay right following signs to the Mount Adams Recreation Area. After heading north for 1.4 miles, the road divides again; stay right. At 2.4 miles the road divides again; stay right on a road signed to the Sno-Parks. Pass the Pine Side Sno-Park at 4.8 miles then continue up the rather rough Forest Road 82 for another 4.4 miles to the end of the plowing at the Smith Butte Sno-Park (3,852 feet). *Note:* The access road to the Sno-Park is not plowed on weekends. Always carry tire chains and a shovel.

A snowy day on route to Gotchen Creek

The Tour: The Sno-Park is located at the intersection of Road 82 and Spur Road (8200)200, which branches off to the right. Your route heads out north from the Sno-Park following Road 82 over gently rolling terrain. This area is not usually groomed for skiers, so early arrivals must be ready to break trail.

After skiing past clearcuts and second growth for ¾ mile the road divides; go left on Spur Road (8225)060, which begins with a short descent then soon levels off into a traverse along the edge of a broad clearcut. At 1 mile you will come to the north end of the clearcut where you will find Spur Road (8225)071. Go right and ski along this road as it cuts along the base of Bunnell Butte, and skirt the northern edge of the broad clearcut before ducking into the forest.

Reach a wide intersection at 2 miles (4,040 feet) and ski to the right on Spur Road (8020)150. You will now begin a steady ascent that will bring you to road's end along the edge of Gotchen Creek at 3¼ miles (4,520 feet).

If you choose to go exploring, continue on from the end of the road and, keeping Gotchen Creek to your left, climb through the sparse forest. Climb until you are tired then turn back for an enjoyable run through the trees.

TROUT LAKE

72 ATKISSON SNO-PARK

Ice Caves Loop

Class: *self-propelled*
Rating: *easiest*
Loop trip: *3¾ mile*
Skiing time: *2 hours*
Elevation gain: *200 feet*
High point: *2,900 feet*
Best: *January–February*
Avalanche potential: *none*
Map: *Green Trails, Willard No. 398*

Peterson Ridge Trail

Class: *self-propelled*
Rating: *more difficult*
Round trip: *9 miles*
Skiing time: *4 hours*
Elevation gain: *940 feet*
High point: *3,640 feet*
Best: *January–mid-March*
Avalanche potential: *low*
Maps: *Green Trails, Willard No. 398
and Mt. Adams West No. 366*

Map on page 188

The roar, the snarl, and the belching exhaust of the snowmobiles at the popular Atkisson Sno-Park is enough to scare away any peace-loving skier. However, if you can get past the noise shock of the parking area, you will find miles of snowmobile-free trails reserved for skiers. In fact, the only thing skiers and snowmobilers share is the parking area, restroom, shelter with picnic tables and a wood stove (bring some wood), a few feet of trail, and a love for winter fun.

Two skier-only tours start from the Sno-Park. The easy Ice Caves Loop explores the forest and clearcuts in the caves area with an optional 3-mile add-on loop around the Natural Bridges area. The second option is a moderately easy climb on a forest road to a view of Mount Hood from a saddle on Peterson Ridge.

Access: From Highway 14 in the Columbia Gorge, head north on Highway 141 for 25 miles to Trout Lake. (If you are coming from the west you may use Alternate Highway 141 and shorten your drive by a couple of miles.) Stay to the left on Highway 141 when the road divides in Trout Lake. You will pass the Mount Adams Ranger Station before you reach the end of the plowed road at 5.8 miles from the intersection. Go left, off the county road for 0.2 miles to the Atkisson Sno-Park parking area (2,700 feet).

Ice Caves Loop: From the Sno-Park follow the snowmobiles into the woods for 30 feet to Spur Road (1400)017. Go left. After 100 feet the snowmobiles will head off to the right (your return route). The Ice Caves Loop heads through the forest on an old road that rolls with the uneven terrain. The tour route passes close to the Ice Caves but does not actually reach them. The Ice Caves are located to the right of the ski route at about ¾ mile from the Sno-Park. Snow-covered stairs and icy footing in the caves make them rather treacherous in the winter.

At the 1½-mile point, the Ice Caves Loop arrives at an intersection. To

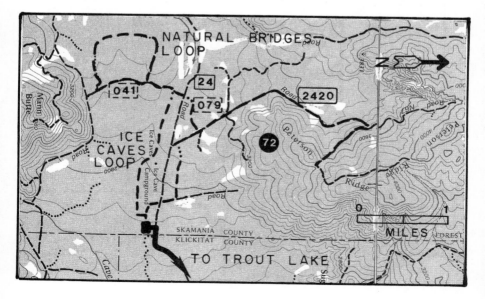

the left, the Natural Bridges Loop allows you to add 3 extra miles to your tour while circling the Big Trench, a collapsed lava tube spanned by several bridges. The trench is very icy in the winter—stay away from the edges.

The Ice Caves Loop goes right at the intersection with the Natural Bridges Loop and soon crosses the snowmobile-groomed Road 24 then heads cross-country for a short distance before turning right on Road (2420)709. At 2½ miles this road ends and the loop route heads right on Peterson Ridge Trail No. 2420. After paralleling a clearcut for ¼ mile, go left across a clearcut.

An ice cave

The loop ends with a right turn that leads to Road 24. Cross the road and continue straight. You will rejoin the snowmobiles for the final ¼ mile of the loop back to the Sno-Park.

Peterson Ridge Trail: This tour can be skied as an extension of the Ice Caves Loop or as an independent tour. If you ski the entire Ice Caves Loop in addition to the Peterson Ridge Trail your total will be 10¼ miles. However, if you head out from the Sno-Park and go right with the snowmobiles, as described below, you can reduce the trip mileage to 9 miles.

From the Sno-Park follow the snowmobiles into the woods for 30 feet then go left for 100 feet before heading to the right on a ¼-mile shared corridor to Road 24. Cross the groomed road and follow the blue diamonds for the next ¾ mile. At 1¼ mile leave the Ice Caves Loop and head straight on Road 2420. The route to the ridge is well marked and easy to follow as it descends briefly to cross Dry Creek then climbs gradually, passing clearcuts and the eastern edge of Lost Meadow. At 4 miles from the Sno-Park, Road 2420 makes a radical turn to the right (3,450 feet) and the final ½ mile is spent traversing then climbing to reach the crest of Peterson Ridge at 4½ miles (3,650 feet). If you have the time and skill you can climb the knoll to the south for better views or head north for further exploration on the roads along the ridge crest.

WIND RIVER

73 McCLELLAN MEADOWS LOOP

Class: groomed
Rating: more difficult
Loop trip: 6 miles
Skiing time: 3 hours
Elevation gain: 420 feet

High point: 3,050 feet
Best: mid-December–February
Avalanche potential: none
Maps: Green Trails, Lone Butte No 365 and Wind River No 397; USFS, Wind River Ranger District

The Wind River Winter Sports Area is better known to Oregon skiers than to skiers from Washington, and that is a shame because it is one of the most intriguing Sno-Park areas in the state. Skiers have a myriad of forest roads to tour starting from eight Sno-Parks. Of these eight Sno-Parks, four are reserved for nonmotorized winter sports.

In the nonmotorized area, skiers will find miles of forest roads groomed and set with tracks as well as miles of nongroomed roads and trails. Tour lengths vary from an easy 1¼-mile romp on the groomed Old Man Loop to the challenging 12½-mile Road 65 Loop, which follows ungroomed roads and summer hiking trails.

The McClellan Meadows Loop is a combination of groomed roads and ungroomed trails. Plenty of opportunities exist for stride and glide–type touring as well as for telemarkers to weave their magic over clearcuts. The skiing on this loop is not difficult, except for a slightly tricky trail descent and one very steep and difficult climb.

Access: From Highway 14 in the Columbia Gorge, head north to the town of Carson, famous for its hot spring and nearby hotel. Continue north from Carson on the Wind River Road (which becomes Forest Road 30). At 21 miles, cross Old Man Pass then descend for a final 2.2 miles to the small Road 3050 Sno-Park (2,898 feet).

The Tour: Start your tour from the west side of Road 30. You will take only a few strides on Road 3050 before arriving at your first intersection. Go left and ski south on the groomed Snow Foot Trail No. 148. The trail heads through the forest for ½ mile to an intersection with the Scenic Trail. Continue straight, following the combined Snow Foot and Scenic Trails on a winding journey through the forest for the next 1½ miles to the Road 3054 Sno-Park.

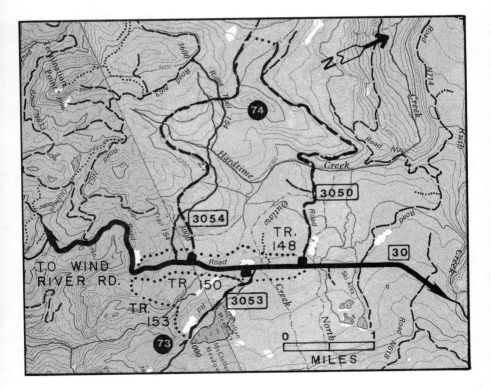

Trail 151 is scenic and a lot of fun to ski.

At the Sno-Park you must leave the Scenic Trail and ski left around the upper end of the parking area to find a trail signed to Old Man Pass. The trail climbs steadily and arrives at 3,050-foot Old Man Pass at 2½ miles. Here you cross to the east side of Road 30 then continue your loop on Trail 151. This is a true trail. It is narrow and ungroomed and leads you directly to adventure by swooping down through a clearcut to cross the Wind River (2,780 feet). The trail then climbs. The upward journey begins with a moderate climbing traverse that turns into a steep scramble up a narrow cut to the top of a 3,000-foot ridge. At 4 miles, Trail 151 intersects the McClellan Meadows Trail and ends. The meadows lie straight ahead through a narrow band of trees but may be difficult to access due to a small creek.

The loop route turns left here and heads northeast on the well-groomed Road 3053 for 1¼ miles to the Road 3053 Sno-Park. There is an intersection just before the Sno-Park; go right for the final ¾ mile on the groomed Hardtime Trail to return to the Road 3050 Sno-Park at 6 miles.

74 HARDTIME LOOP

Class: *groomed*
Rating: *more difficult*
Loop trip: *10½ miles*
Skiing time: *5 hours*
Elevation gain: *580 feet*

High point: *3,280 feet*
Best: *mid-December–mid-March*
Avalanche potential: *none*
Maps: *Green Trails, Wind River No. 397 and Lone Butte No. 365; USFS, Wind River Ranger District*

Map on page 191

The name Hardtime in no way describes the conditions encountered while skiing this easy-going, immaculately groomed loop. In fact, except when the snow is extremely icy, this loop could be rated as easiest.

Pack an extra-heavy lunch for this long loop, and be sure to add your camera to the top of your pack. On a clear day you will view countless cinder cones, the Indian Heaven Wilderness, the endless forest plantations of the Gifford Pinchot National Forest, miles of open ridges that are part of the Mount St. Helens devastation area, and the three giants—the lordly Mount Rainier, the domineering Mount Adams, and the rather truncated Mount St. Helens.

Access: From Highway 14 in the Columbia River Gorge, head north to the town of Carson then continue north on the Wind River Road. After 7 miles the Wind River Road becomes Forest Road 30. Continue straight for another 14 miles to Old Man Pass (3,050 feet) then descend 1.6 miles to the Road 3053 Sno-Park, located on the right-hand side of the road (2,900 feet).

The Tour: From the Road 3053 Sno-Park, walk past the information board then ski into the woods for 20 feet to intersect the Hardtime Loop. For now go right; you will return to this point on the trail to your left. The trail is groomed and stays in the forest while gradually climbing for the next 1½ miles to the crest of the 3,050-foot summit of Old Man Pass. At the pass you must cross to the west side of Road 30 then ski into the woods.

As you head through the trees you will pass several well-signed intersections—stay left. The Hardtime Loop is joined by the Scenic Loop, and together the two loops head up a groomed logging road. The Indian Heaven Wilderness comes into view as you reach the first large clearcut at 2¼ miles. At 3¼ miles reach the end of the second large clearcut (at least it was the second in 1994) where the Scenic Loop branches off to the right. The Hardtime Loop continues straight ahead. A short descent leads to a crossing of Hardtime Creek followed by more gradual climbing.

A mid-week trip on the Hardtime Loop; grooming is done on weekends only

At 6¼ miles, shortly after the first brisk ascent of the tour, the loop route leaves Road 3054 and heads into the trees following a line of blue diamond markers. This portion of the loop is not groomed, but the markers and nearly level terrain ensure an easy crossing to the next road. This pleasant interlude ends at 6½ miles when the trail meets Road 3050 (3,200 feet).

Go right and ski down groomed tracks on Road 3050. In the next mile you will find several enjoyable descents through the forest. The road then traverses several scenic clearcuts with views of Mount St. Helens, Mount Rainier, and Mount Adams. At 8½ miles recross Hardtime Creek (2,700 feet) then begin a gradual but steady climb to Road 30 (2,898 feet). At 10 miles recross Road 30, then follow the rolling Hardtime Trail for the final ¾ mile to close the loop at the Road 3053 Sno-Park at 10½ miles.

75 JUNE LAKE LOOP

June Lake

Class: self-propelled
Rating: more difficult
Round trip: 4½ miles
Skiing time: 3 hours
Elevation gain: 460 feet
High point: 3,100 feet
Best: January–February
Avalanche potential: none
Map: Green Trails, Mount
   St. Helens NW No. 364S

The Loop

Class: self-propelled
Rating: most difficult
Round trip: 5 miles
Skiing time: 3 hours
Elevation gain: 560 feet
High point: 3,200 feet
Best: January–February
Avalanche potential: low
Map: Green Trails, Mount
   St. Helens NW No. 364S

Map on page 196

June Lake is a four-star destination reached by a challenging trail. The rewards are a lake, waterfall, unlimited views of snow-covered Mount St. Helens, sheltered campsites, and a loop for those inclined.

Access: Exit Interstate 5 at Woodland and drive east on State Route 503 for 28.8 miles to Cougar. Go straight through town and continue east for another 6.8 miles, then turn left on Forest Road 83. In 3 miles the road divides; stay right on Road 83 for another 2.7 miles to the huge Marble Mountain Sno-Park at the end of the plowing (2,640 feet).

The Tour: From the Sno-Park there are three ways to cover the ¾ mile to the June Lake Trailhead. The easiest is to join the snowmobiles and ski groomed Road 83 for ¾ mile. The road is accessed from the northern end of the lower side of the parking area. Pine Martin Trail No. 245 is a delightful, skier-only route, which starts from the northern end of the upper side of the parking loop then stays in the trees as it parallels Road 83 for 1 mile. When the trail ends, go left and ski the road over the Lake Creek road bridge to find a large sign marking the June Lake Trailhead on your left (2,700 feet). Your third option is to follow the Wapiti Loop Trails, located on the south side of Road 83, to the June Lake Trailhead. If you choose this option, be sure to pick up a map at the warming hut before you head out.

Once you reach the June Lake Trail, follow the well-marked route up an old clearcut first on road then on a broad trail. Ahead, Mount St. Helens is in full view. At 2⅛ miles from the Sno-Park, enter the Mount St. Helens National Volcanic Monument just as the trail makes a short, steep drop to a small logging platform. There is a short climb followed by a bridge, then

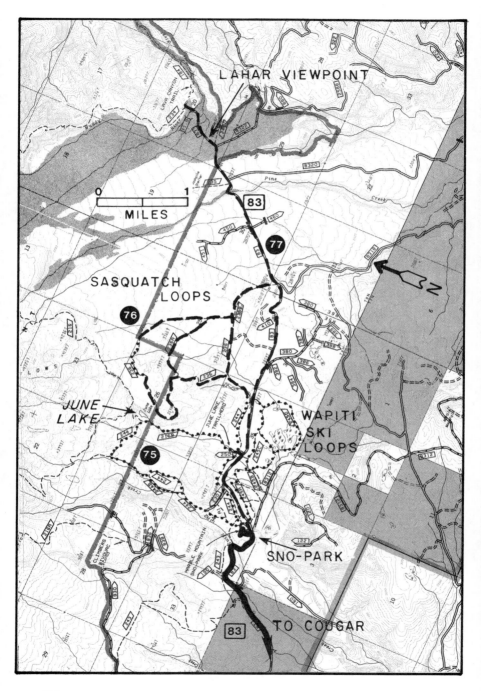

LAHAR VIEWPOINT

83

77

SASQUATCH
LOOPS

76

JUNE
LAKE

WAPITI
SKI
LOOPS

75

SNO-PARK

83   TO COUGAR

0   MILES   1

Skier crossing a bridge near June Lake

you ski out onto an open bench. June Lake and the waterfall are to your right, bounded by steep cliffs (3,100 feet). The level area near the lake offers excellent campsites. Stay back from the edge of the lake, as it is difficult to determine where the lakeshore starts in this broad, flat field of snow.

Skiers opting to make the loop should climb the open slope beyond the lake, heading toward the mountain. (This route is marked.) Near the top of the slope go left and ski down to a small wooded bench (good campsites). Cross the bench and climb up and over a steep rib, angling toward the mountain.

At ½ mile from June Lake is the Swift Creek Skier Trail (a narrow corridor through the forest well marked by blue diamonds). If you followed the Swift Creek Skier Trail to the right from the intersection, you would be on the climbers' route up the mountain. The loop route turns left and descends Trail 244 down the Swift Creek valley. The trail divides twice, giving you options for more challenging descents on Trails 244C and 244B. The ski trail joins a snowmobile road shortly before the parking area.

76 SASQUATCH LOOPS

Middle Loop

Class: *self-propelled*
Rating: *more difficult*
Round trip: *6½ miles*
Skiing time: *3 hours*
Elevation gain: *500 feet*
High point: *3,200 feet*
Best: *January–February*
Avalanche potential: *low*
Map: *Green Trails, Mount St. Helens NW No. 364S*

Map on page 196

Long Loop

Class: *self-propelled*
Rating: *most difficult*
Round trip: *8 miles*
Skiing time: *4 hours*
Elevation gain: *740 feet*
High point: *3,440 feet*
Best: *January–February*
Avalanche potential: *low*
Map: *Green Trails, Mount St. Helens NW No. 364S*

For the views, for the challenge, and for the pure joy of skiing—the Sasquatch Loops take you away from the noise and hustle of the snow-machines, away from the crowds of fellow skiers, and out into the quiet forest plantations at the base of Mount St. Helens.

If the loops are skied in a clockwise direction, you will climb the steepest sections of the trail and find all descents to be gradual. (If you are looking for a challenge, reverse the loop.) The skiing difficulties encountered on the Long Loop are much the same as those encountered on the Middle Loop. The major problems of the Long Loop stem from routefinding rather then skier ability. The blue diamonds that mark the route of the Long Loop are often snow-covered or completely missing, demanding considerable luck and routefinding skills to make your way around the entire route.

Access: Drive to the Marble Mountain Sno-Park (2,640 feet) as described in Tour 75.

The Tour: From the upper end of the parking area ski Pine Martin Trail No. 245 for 1¾ miles to its end at the base of the Sasquatch Loops. The trail cuts through the thick forest and can be slow going, so if you are short on time or low on energy you may join the snowmobiles and ski Road 83 for 1½ miles from the Sno-Park to the start of the Sasquatch Loops (2,763 feet).

The Sasquatch Loops start on the left side of Road 83 a few feet from the end of the Pine Martin Trail. Ski to the large brown map board that marks the trailhead then head uphill for ¼ mile to an intersection and the start of the loop portion of the tour (2,870 feet). Take the left fork and head through a band of trees to an open basin. The trail contours around the basin and begins climbing rapidly along an old road that cuts across the steep hillside. At 2¾ miles from the Sno-Park the trail reaches the crest of a ridge and intersects a wide logging road (3,280 feet).

The Middle and Long Loops separate here. Middle Loop Trail No. 236A heads to the right following the road on a mile-long descending traverse to the east. Trail 236A ends at the 3¾-mile point. Go right on Trail 236 for ¼ mile to an intersection with Trail 236B (3,020 feet) and go right again for a gradual descent back to the start of the loop portion of the tour at 4¾ miles. Go left to return to Road 83 at 5 miles.

The Long Loop goes left from the Middle Loop Trail intersection and contours around the ridge to views of Marble Mountain and Mount Adams. Past a weather station the road swings west around the ridge to a view of the Worm Flows on the side of Mount St. Helens.

Your routefinding difficulties begin when the road ends (3,430 feet). Continue straight ahead on a rough trail, marked with blue diamonds, which traverses around the hillside then descends to a broad, flat ridge top. Head straight across the open ridge top. About half of the way across the trail disappears. At this point you should angle off to your left. You will find the trail again about 200 feet from the wall of trees along the northwest side of a clearcut. Parallel the trees until you find a narrow road.

Head down the narrow road until you reach an intersection at 4¼ miles from the Sno-Park. Go left and descend at a steady rate down a road that serves as a riverbed during spring runoff. Stay to the right as you follow

Trail marked with blue diamonds on the Long Loop

the deep road/river trench until you rejoin Middle Loop Trail No. 236A at 5¼ miles. Continue down for ¼ mile to reach the Trail 236B intersection. Go right on Trail 236B to reach the end of the loop portion of your tour at 6 miles. Retrace you tracks back to Road 83. To return to the Sno-Park you may ski the road (quickest), return via Pine Martin Trail No. 245, or, if you are looking for fun, cross Road 83 and wander through the Wapiti Loops.

77 LAHAR VIEWPOINT

Class: *multiple use*
Rating: *easiest*
Round trip: *9¼ miles*
Skiing time: *5 hours*
Elevation gain: *410 feet*

High point: *2,930 feet*
Best: *mid-December–March*
Avalanche potential: *none*
Map: *Green Trails, Mt. St. Helens No. 364*

Map on page 196

An early start will help you avoid the rush along this popular shared road to a spectacular view of Mount St. Helens. The destination is a broad mud-flow that is a beautiful, open, snow-covered plain in the winter. This vast open plain rises to the gleaming slopes of the mountain and the overall result is an ice sculpture that would win first prize in any contest.

On the weekends snowshoers, hikers, and an endless stream of snowmobilers share this tour with the skiers. The snowmobilers use the road as an access to the mudflow where they are free to head across the open slopes, climbing to the Plains of Abraham and on to a view over Spirit Lake from Windy Ridge.

Skiers may avoid much of the noise and smell by spending the first and last portion the tour on skier-only trails. Skiing these trails is neither as quick nor as easy as following the groomed road used by the snowmobiles, but it is a whole lot more peaceful.

Access: Drive to the Marble Mountain Sno-Park (2,640 feet), as described in Tour 75.

The Tour: If you have beginners in your party or are getting the suggested early start, then begin your tour by skiing up Road 83. You may access this road by the snowmobile ramp located at the upper end of the lower side of the parking loop. Road 83 is then followed for 4½ miles to the Lahar area where you leave the forest and enter the open plain (2,930 feet). When you are done staring at Mount St. Helens, look for Mount Adams to the east and Mount Hood to the south.

Skiing on the open plains of the mudflow below Mount St. Helens

If you choose to avoid the road, walk the upper end of the parking loop and scramble up the bank to find the start of Pine Martin Trail No. 245. This trail parallels Road 83 for 1¾ miles, passing the start of the Swift Creek Trail and the June Lake Trail before it ends at the Sasquatch Trailhead. You can continue to avoid the road by following Sasquatch Trail No. 236. You will add an extra mile to your trip length and an extra ½ hour of skiing time. Ski up Sasquatch Trail No. 236 for ¼ mile to the first intersection then go right, heading up a low hill for ½ mile to a second intersection. Continue straight, on rarely used Trail 236B, which heads north to end at Road 83 at the 3¼-mile point. Go left for the final 2 miles to the Lahar area.

Once you reach the open plains of the mudflow, descend to the intersection and head left, still following Road 83. The groomer does not go here and neither do the majority of the snowmobiles. You can angle down and across the plains for ¾ mile to reach road's end at Lava Canyon. Do not venture out on the trails in this scenic area; they are steep, slippery, and very hazardous when snow-covered.

If you armed yourself with a map before starting out, try the Wapiti Ski Loops on the way back. These trails may be accessed from Road 83, opposite the start of the Sasquatch Trails. The Wapiti Ski Loops will bring you back to the Marble Mountain Sno-Park after some pleasant meandering through the forest and meadows.

78 MOUNT ST. HELENS

Class: *self-propelled*
Rating: *mountaineer*
Round trip: *8 miles*
Skiing time: *8 hours*
Elevation gain: *5,725 feet via Worm Flows*

High point: *8,365 feet*
Best: *January–May*
Avalanche potential: *moderate*
Map: *Green Trails, Mount. St. Helens NW No. 364S*

Mount St. Helens, or what remains of it, is a telemarkers' haven. The slopes are fairly uniform and when the sun softens the snow they are skiable by any competent kick-turner.

But skiing Mount St. Helens is not a cakewalk. When the snows refuse to soften, the icy slopes are a horror to three-pinners, and nasty, even fatal slips are possible. In addition, there are dangers to skiing any major peak that demands the skill and judgment of experienced mountaineers.

Skiing above 4,800 feet on Mount St. Helens requires a permit. An unlimited number of these permits are self-issued daily between November 1 and May 15. From May 16 through October, however, only 40 permits are issued per day; 30 of these permits may be reserved in advance by writing to Mount St. Helens Volcanic National Monument Headquarters, Route 1, Box 269, Amboy, WA 98601. The remaining 10 permits are available at Jacks Restaurant in Yale on a first-come first-served basis on the day of the tour. When volcanic hazard is high, no permits are issued.

Access: Exit Interstate 5 at Woodland. Drive east on State Route 503 for 24.1 miles to Yale and register. Drive on, passing through Cougar after 4.7 miles to reach an intersection at 11.5 miles. Turn left on Forest Road 83 and drive 3 miles to the Cougar Sno-Park and a choice. In midwinter, when there is still plenty of snow, you should go right and follow Road 83 for another 2.7 miles to the Marble Mountain Sno-Park (2,640 feet) and ski the Worm Flows Route. In the late spring you should go left and drive up Forest Road 81 for 1.7 miles, then go right on Spur Road 830 for 2.7 steep miles up to a dry camping area known as the Climbers Bivouac (3,700 feet).

The Worm Flows: The tour begins from the upper side of the parking loop, just above the warming hut. Climb the snowmobile ramp and head into the trees for 20 feet to the first intersection. Go straight and follow the blue diamonds through the forest to Swift Creek Ski Trail No. 244. At ¼ mile Trail 244B branches off to the left. Either Trail 244 or 244B may be used; Trail 244 is the easiest. Follow either trail to its intersection with Trail 244A, an old logging road, then go left and climb steadily up the Swift Creek valley.

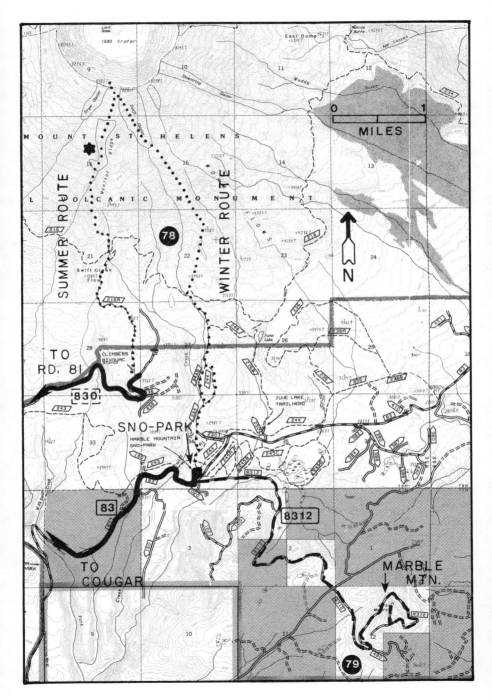

203

Ascending Monitor Ridge; Mount Hood in distance

Near the 1-mile point the trail divides again. Both trails go to the same place, so take either the steeper Trail 244C on the left or stick with Trail 244 and continue the ascent. Shortly after the two trails rejoin, you will reach the June Lake Trail intersection at 2¼ miles (3,500 feet). Continue straight along the snow-covered ridge. The climb abates as you leave the trees then increases as you cross Swift Creek and head toward the base of the mountain.

At 2¾ miles (3,800 feet) pass the last campsites and begin the long haul up the mountain. Pick an elevated area for your ascent, following the twisty turns of one of the Worm Flows to the crest of Monitor Ridge, which you reach at around the 7,200-foot level. Once on the ridge angle a bit to the west for your final push to the 8,300-foot crater rim. The actual 8,365-foot high point is located ¾ mile to the west. Use extreme caution as you approach the crater rim. A huge, 50-foot cornice usually extends off the rim over the crater. Posts have been placed to let you know where the rim is. If the posts are covered with snow, stay way back from the edge.

The Summer Route: By May the snow has usually melted to the point where the best skiing is found on the summer route. From the Climbers Bivouac follow Ptarmigan Trail No. 216A to timberline. Once out of the trees turn right and follow a gully up to a small bench (4,800 feet) where the real climb begins. Ski west, climbing a steepish slope to the ridge top, then head north toward the crater rim, skiing up a series of narrow gullies and ribs on the west side of Monitor Ridge. At 6,200 feet the last gully peters out and a steep (often icy) slope must be cautiously traversed or avoided by dropping below it. When the snow is unstable the slope should be completely avoided by climbing to the ridge above and following the exposed rocks to the main snow slopes.

Once the steep slope is traversed, climb to the right (east), following the natural roll of the terrain up Monitor Ridge to the crest at 7,200 feet. On the left, skirt a large bowl, which is prone to avalanche when the snow is unstable. Once on the ridge, turn north and ski the open slopes toward the crater.

COUGAR

79 MARBLE MOUNTAIN

Class: multiple use
Rating: more difficult
Round trip: 11 miles
Skiing time: 6 hours
Elevation gain: 1,488 feet

High point: 4,128 feet
Best: January–mid-March
Avalanche potential: low
Map: Green Trails, Mount St. Helens No. 364

Map on page 203

A full day of views and a delightful tour await all skiers willing to brave the snowmobiles on Marble Mountain.

Access: Drive to the Marble Mountain Sno-Park on Forest Road 83 (2,640 feet; see Tour 75 for directions).

The Tour: Walk back to the Sno-Park entrance. Pass gated Road 83 on the left and descend a few more feet to find the Road 8312 gate also on the left. Put your skis on here and start your tour with an easy downhill glide on the snowmobile-groomed Road 8312. The gradual descent takes you past an entrance to the Wapiti Ski Loops then continues down to cross a small stream. At ¾ mile the road starts to climb.

The climb is steady, traversing into a small side valley, then abruptly turning east to open slopes. Starting at 2 miles are tremendous views of the south side of Mount St. Helens from the crater rim down the gleaming white slopes, through the Worm Flows formations to the forest below.

At 2¾ miles, cross through a shallow pass and head southeast, still climbing to reach the Four-Corners junction in another ¼ mile (3,360 feet). Continue straight ahead over broad, rolling clearcut slopes. Here the road levels and it's time to practice skating on the snowmobile-packed surface (this portion of the road is not always groomed).

The road starts to climb again near 4¼ miles, wrapping its way to the 4,128-foot summit of Marble Mountain and views of Mount St. Helens, Mount Adams, Mount Rainier, Mount Hood, and Mount Jefferson, Swift Reservoir, endless clearcuts, roads, and forests. (On a clear day you may prefer to cut a mile from the total by leaving Road 8312 at the summit and descending west to rejoin the road below.)

View of Mount St. Helens near Four-Corners junction

Snowmobiles are in evidence on this road nearly every day. Although the road is too short for the machines to get in a full day's exercise, the open meadows above the 3-mile point draw them in. Start your trip early, but not too early to miss their antics as they turn around in the limited space found at the summit. If you feel that snowmobiles do not belong on this road, please send a letter to District Ranger, Mount St. Helens National Volcanic Monument, Amboy, WA 98601.

80 MOUNT WASHINGTON

Class: *multiple use*
Rating: *more difficult*
Round trip: *up to 14 miles*
Skiing time: *3–6 hours*
Elevation gain: *2,700 feet*

High point: *3,600 feet*
Best: *January–March*
Avalanche potential: *moderate*
Map: *Custom Correct, Mount Skokomish–Lake Cushman*

On a sunny day the scenery can't be beat. Ski the Big Creek Road for miles as it wanders along slopes of 5,944-foot Mount Ellinor and its nextdoor neighbor, 6,255-foot Mount Washington. Gaze out over Hood Canal and Puget Sound to Mount Rainier.

Access: Drive to Hoodsport on Highway 101 then head west on Lake Cushman Road for 9 miles to the end of pavement; go right 1.5 miles on Road 24, then left on Big Creek Road No. 2419 to the snowline—wherever that may be as dictated by the mood of the season and the mood of the day.

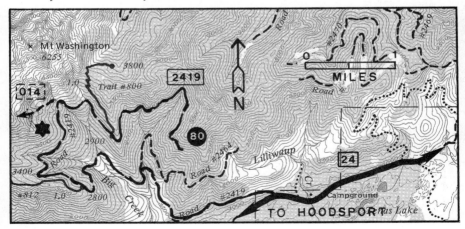

Mount Washington from Big Creek Road

The Tour: Since a party won't know in advance how far it can drive, the trip plan must be flexible. Road 2419 starts at an elevation of 900 feet and goes nearly 7 miles to end in a clearcut at 3,510 feet. It may therefore be a 14-mile day—or much less, depending.

The road sets out from 900 feet in a steady climb for the first 2½ miles, the angle easing off as a spur road is passed. Big Creek is crossed at 3 miles and a long traverse begins along the side of Mount Washington. At 3½ miles a short spur leads to a clearcut with a broad vista over Lake Cushman and Prospect Ridge. At 3¾ miles pass the Mount Ellinor Trailhead (3,500 feet); the lower stretch of this trail is wooded, narrow, and steep, and the upper portion has avalanche hazard, so skiing is not recommended.

At 4½ miles the road splits. The left fork, Spur Road 014, goes to a clearcut where the upper Mount Ellinor Trailhead is located. In midwinter, or when snow is unstable, this is a good turnaround–picnic spot (3,600 feet) with excellent views of Lake Cushman.

For broader views of Puget Sound waterways and cities as well as a panoramic look at the Cascades, continue on Road 2419, which gains very little elevation as it traverses beneath steep—and avalanche-prone—slopes of Mount Washington to the Mount Washington Trailhead. The road then bears eastward along a ridge, rounds a corner, heads north, and at 7 miles reaches a clearcut and views (3,510 feet). The road continues on, but now it heads down, so turn around here and enjoy your cruise back.

81 FOUR STREAM ROAD

Class: *multiple use*
Rating: *more difficult*
Round trip: *up to 9 miles*
Skiing time: *up to 5 hours*
Elevation gain: *up to 1,800 feet*

High point: *3,000 feet*
Best: *January–mid-March*
Avalanche potential: *low*
Maps: *Custom Correct, Enchanted*
Valley–Skokomish

Ski from the shores of Lake Cushman up through virgin-timbered National Park and clearcut National Forest to a view of the southern Olympics rarely seen except by loggers.

Access: From Hoodsport on Highway 101 drive Lake Cushman Road 9 miles to the end of pavement. Stay left and head along the lakeshore on Road 24 for 5 miles, to near the head of the lake. Go left on Four Stream Road No. 2451, which quickly crosses the North Fork Skokomish River, the base point

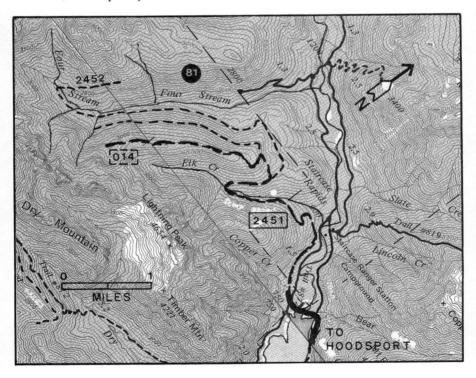

Mount Lincoln (on the right) from Four Stream Road

of this trip (800 feet). Continue driving Road 2451 to the snowline, which is a mile or two from the river except in periods of unusually deep snow.

The Tour: Four Stream Road climbs steeply and narrowly from the valley floor, blasted from the rocky hillside. At 1½ miles enter Olympic National Park and at 2½ miles leave it at the beginning of a succession of clearcuts. Cross Elk Creek beneath a cliffy shoulder of Lightning Peak then northeast for views of Mount Pershing, Mount Washington, Mount Ellinor, and Copper Mountain.

At 4 miles the road splits. The right fork wanders on for miles through the Four Stream drainage. Ski left on Road (2451)014 for the big views. In a scant ½ mile go left to the ridge top and get out the lunch.

Looking up the North Fork Skokomish, count the valleys on the west side; the valley below you is Four Stream, the next is Five Stream, then Six, Seven, Eight, and Nine, all about a mile apart. North and east are the rugged summits of Mount Lincoln and Copper Mountain, wearing their white winter overcoats. South is Lightning Peak, its imposing cliffs making it seem much higher than 4,654 feet.

Before returning, try a few downhill runs in the clearcuts.

82 MOUNT TOWNSEND

Class: *multiple use*
Rating: *more difficult*
Round trip: *7 miles*
Skiing time: *4 hours*
Elevation gain: *875 feet*

High point: *3,900 feet*
Best: *January–March*
Avalanche potential: *low*
Map: *Custom Correct, Buckhorn Wilderness*

Steep, rugged terrain and gated roads combine to make winter access to high country of the Olympics nearly impossible. However, at the northern end of the range is one outstanding exception where open logging roads pass below the white ramparts of Mount Townsend to overlooks of Puget Sound and volcanoes of the Cascades. Trip possibilities are numerous, ranging from half-day tours to overlooks or a backpack to a little lake.

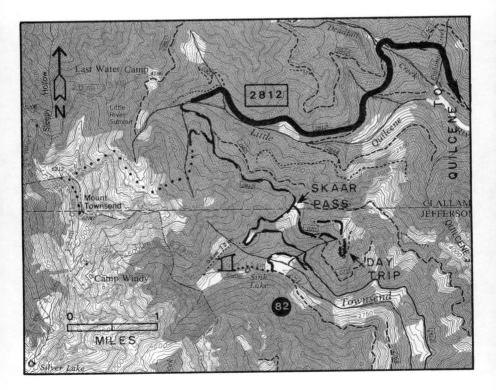

Access: From Quilcene, drive Highway 101 north 1.5 miles. Turn left on Lords Lake Road for 2.9 miles. Just before the lake, turn left on Road 2909 for 3.6 miles to a major intersection. Take the extreme left fork and head downhill on Road 2812. In 0.5 mile is another junction; stay on Road 2812 as it turns right, heading up the Little Quilcene River Valley toward Mount Townsend. The tour starts at the Little Quilcene River bridge (3,025 feet). (After heavy snowfalls be prepared to start skiing lower—perhaps from Highway 101.)

The Tour: Cross the bridge and ski 2 miles along clearcut slopes in an ever-growing panorama of the Cascades from Glacier Peak to Mount Baker. At Skaar Pass (3,700 feet) the view extends to include Mount Rainier.

View seekers should take the second spur road to the left, located near the crest of the pass. Ski 1 mile east, climbing and traversing to the summit of a 3,900-foot knoll to an overlook of Hood Canal and island-dotted Puget Sound.

For longer trips descend from Skaar Pass, dropping 1,000 feet of elevation in 3 miles to Townsend Creek. Follow the Mount Townsend Trail ½ mile, gaining 150 feet to reach a small three-sided shelter in the flats of Sink Lake (2,950 feet).

Mount Townsend

83 OBSTRUCTION POINT

Waterhole Camp

Class: self-propelled
Rating: most difficult
Round trip: 7 miles
Skiing time: 5 hours
Elevation gain: 200 feet
High point: 5,000 feet
Best: January–April
Avalanche potential: low
Map: Custom Correct, Hurricane
Ridge

Obstruction Point

Class: self-propelled
Rating: backcountry
Round trip: 16 miles
Skiing time: 2 days
Elevation gain: 1,300 feet
High point: 6,200 feet
Best: January–April
Avalanche potential: low
Map: Custom Correct, Hurricane
Ridge

Map on page 214

The Obstruction Point Trail avoids the crowds of Hurricane Hill (Tour 84) and leads to excellent skiing in winter beauty and solitude. Day-trippers can enjoy a tour to Waterhole Camp; overnighters can make the panoramic beauty of Obstruction Point their goal.

Access: From Port Angeles drive 17 miles to Hurricane Ridge. Before setting out, register your tour at the Visitor Center. Drive back down the road 0.3 mile from the Visitor Center to a small parking area at the last major turn of the highway (4,900 feet). (The trailhead is located just above the new sledding area.)

The Tour: The route follows the narrow Obstruction Point Road, which begins with a steep descending traverse along the exposed hillside. The rapid descent continues until the road reaches the crest of a forested ridge. You then traverse rolling, forested terrain, breaking into the open at 1½ miles on the south side of Steeple Rock. Views extend over the Bailey Range and

Ski tracks on the open slopes near Obstruction Point

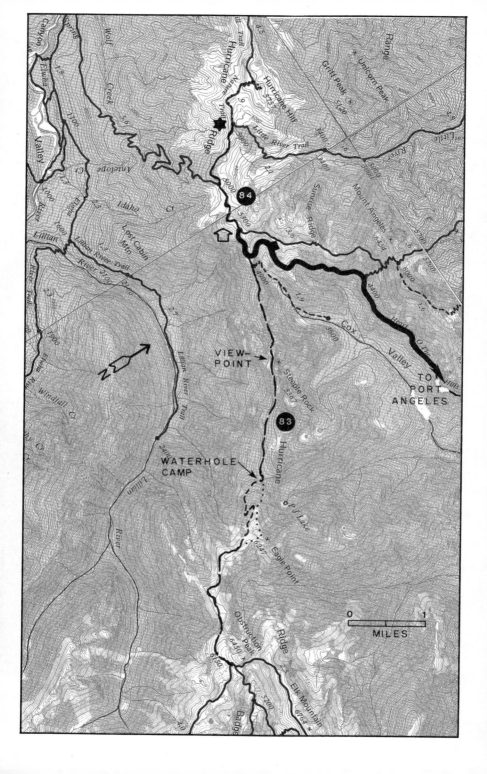

the Alaskan-looking, 7,965-foot lord of the area, Mount Olympus. If the snow is icy or the weather is bad, make the edge of the clearing the turnaround.

Beyond the clearing the road reenters forest, traverses two more small hills, and at 3½ miles reaches forested Waterhole Camp (5,000 feet), a good turnaround for day skiers—keep in mind that the road back to Port Angeles is gated at dusk.

Waterhole Camp offers the last well-protected campsites on this tour. Ski to your right to find the outhouse and left or right of the road for level campsites. If the weather is stable and you trust your local weather reporter, you may want to continue on and find a camp on the open slopes above.

The road now climbs, gaining 750 feet in the next 1½ miles while traversing the south side of 6,247-foot Eagle Point. The last 3 miles to Obstruction Point cross open meadows above treeline, exposing skiers to grand views, sometimes dangerously icy hills, and perhaps bad weather. The final mile climbs to the end of Obstruction Point Road (6,150 feet), with excellent views and campsites. Travel beyond the point is not recommended due to high avalanche potential.

At the end of your tour, be sure to return to the Visitor Center to sign out on the register.

Steeple Rock and Eagle Point from Hurricane Ridge

84 HURRICANE HILL

Ridge Road

Class: self-propelled
Rating: more difficult
Round trip: 3 miles
Skiing time: 2 hours
Elevation gain: 200 feet
High point: 5,200 feet
Best: January–mid-April
Avalanche potential: none
Map: Custom Correct, Hurricane Ridge

Hilltop

Class: self-propelled
Rating: backcountry
Round trip: 6 miles
Skiing time: 4 hours
Elevation gain: 760 feet
High point: 5,757 feet
Best: January–mid-April
Avalanche potential: moderate
Map: Custom Correct, Hurricane Ridge

Map on page 214

Don't expect to be alone amid scenery that led the United Nations to designate Olympic National Park a World Heritage Park. In good weather throngs of nordic skiers swarm the unplowed road from Hurricane Ridge Visitor Center to Hurricane Hill. "Hurricane" is a deserved name and often the road is deeply scooped by wind cirques.

From the end of the road, *backcountry* skiers may continue cross-country to the summit of Hurricane Hill for more views and glorious telemark descents of the steep bowls.

Access: From Port Angeles drive 17 miles to Hurricane Ridge. Register your trip destination at the Visitor Center (5,200 feet).

The Tour: Ski west from the lodge, skirting the downhill ski area, following the route of the snow-covered road. The road is easy to follow once it enters the trees and begins its descent along the ridge crest. At 1 mile the road levels, passes the picnic area, then climbs a bit to the road end at 1½ miles.

A skiers' information board at the end of the road marks the turnaround point for most skiers. Beyond here it is a difficult 1½-mile climb to the crest of Hurricane Hill. From this point on, competence in telemarking and/or kick-turning is essential. So is an eye for the weather, which in an hour can change from balmy sunshine to blinding blizzards. Be prepared for a quick retreat.

Part of the way is on a very narrow ridge with a knife-edge crest. Stay atop the ridge and climb over a small knoll rather than trying to traverse its very steep and dangerous sides; in unstable or icy conditions this is mandatory. Ski down the far side of the knoll, wary of cornices on the north (right), then around a second knoll to the foot of Hurricane Hill.

A rock outcrop amid stunted, wind-blasted trees marks the 5,757-foot summit. Gaze over Port Angeles, the Strait of Juan de Fuca, Victoria, Vancouver Island mountains, the British Columbia Coast Range, and, of course, Mount Baker. Reach for another sandwich and turn to gaze over the Elwha Valley and Bailey Range to Olympus.

Mount Olympus (center) from Hurricane Hill

AND MORE SKI TOURS

The 84 ski tours covered in this book barely scratch the surface of the skiing opportunities in the South Cascades and Olympics. The following is a list of other public places to explore as well as two excellent commercial areas.

Snoqualmie Pass

Ski Acres Cross-Country Ski Center: The 37 miles (60 km) of beautifully groomed trails for diagonal striding and skating in an outstandingly scenic setting make this the foremost cross-country area in the southern half of the Cascades. Beginners will find great skiing on the lower trails while the more experienced may ride the chairlift up to the challenging trails above. In addition, there is a downhill area for telemarkers. Lessons, ski rentals, food service, warming huts, and night skiing are available. Fee charged.

Cabin Creek: Groomed trails for diagonal striding and skating are located on the east side of Interstate 90 at the base of Amabilis Mountain. The 6 miles (10 km) of trails range from *easiest* on level forest roads to *more difficult* on steep clearcut hillsides. These trails are part of the Trollhaugen Hut system (a cross-country ski racers club). The grooming is done by Sno-Park funds and the trails are open to all except on race days.

Swauk Pass Highway 97

Swauk Campground Sno-Park: Located 25 miles east of Cle Elum on Highway 97. The campground has the added advantage of having toilets and a kitchen.

White River

West Fork White River: Spring skiing and excellent views from roads and clearcuts on Frog Mountain once the West Fork Road is open. Access is 3 miles south of the town of Greenwater on Highway 410.

Suntop Sno-Park: Road 73 is groomed for 5 miles (8 km) from the Sno-Park. For more information see Tour 33.

Naches River

Nile Creek Road: Best for early- or late-season skiing when the road is open as far as the feed station. Destination and miles variable. Access is from Highway 410 at the town of Nile.

American River

Blankenship Meadows: A 7-mile ski trail to meadows and lakes below Tumac Mountain for experienced backcountry skiers. Access is from Bumping Lake (Tour 67). Tour starts by skiing around the west side of the lake.

Mount Rainier

Nisqually Vista: A ¾-mile round trip on marked trail. Good views of mountain and glacier. Rated easiest by the Park Service but very steep in sections. Access begins behind the Paradise Visitor Center.

White Pass

White Pass Ski Area: The 9 miles (15 km) of groomed ski trails on the north side of White Pass are part of the White Pass Ski Area concession. The trails loop around White Pass (Leech) Lake then head east over rolling terrain through forest and meadows. A use fee is charged.

Goose Egg: A 4¼-mile round trip on level terrain along the Tieton River makes this an ideal trip for the beginning skier. Because of the low-elevation start (2,600 feet), plan to ski here in January and February only. The tour starts from the Goose Egg Sno-Park (see Tour 62 for details).

Goldendale

Satus Pass: Located on the west side of the pass, 11 miles north of Goldendale, this is a relatively unknown Sno-Park. Skiers and snowmobiles share the forest road, which runs along the ridge crest at the edge of the Yakima Indian Reservation. Although skiing starts at 3,150 feet, snow rarely lingers on these hill after February.

Olympics

Hamma Hamma River Road: Low-elevation valley-bottom tour. As much as 10 miles of skiable road each way. Access is from Highway 101, 2 miles north of Eldon.

Dosewallips River Road: Low-elevation valley-bottom skiing past falls to road-end (5–10 miles from snowline). Access is off Highway 101 just north of Dosewallips State Park.

SUGGESTED READING

Avalanche Safety

Fraser, Colin. *Avalanches and Snow Safety.* New York: Charles Scribner's Sons, 1978.

Graydon, Don, ed. *Mountaineering: The Freedom of the Hills,* 5th ed. Seattle: The Mountaineers, 1982.

LaChappelle, E. R. *ABC of Avalanche Safety,* 2d ed. Seattle: The Mountaineers, 1985.

Enjoying the Outdoors (Proper Clothing, Ski Equipment, Winter Camping)

Brady, Michael. *Cross-Country Ski Gear,* 2d ed. Seattle: The Mountaineers, 1988.

Tejada-Flores, Lito. *Backcountry Skiing.* San Francisco: Sierra Club Books, 1981.

Watters, Ron. *Ski Camping.* San Francisco: Chronicle Books, 1979.

How To

Barnett, Steve. *Cross-Country Downhill,* 2d ed. Seattle: Pacific Search Press, 1979.

Bein, Vic. *Mountain Skiing.* Seattle: The Mountaineers, 1982.

Gilette, Ned, and John Dostal. *Cross-Country Skiing,* 3d ed. Seattle: The Mountaineers, 1988.

First Aid

Lentz, Martha, Steven Macdonald, and Jan Carline. *Mountaineering First Aid,* 3d ed. Seattle: The Mountaineers, 1985.

Wilkerson, James A., M.D., ed. *Medicine for Mountaineering,* 3d ed. Seattle: The Mountaineers, 1985.

INDEX

ABOUT THE AUTHORS

Vicky Spring and Tom Kirkendall are both experienced outdoor people. The couple travel the hills in summer as hikers, backpackers, and cyclists on mountain bikes; when the snow falls, they pin on cross-country skis and keep on exploring. Both Tom and Vicky studied at the Brooks Institute of Photography in Santa Barbara, California, and are now building their careers together as outdoor photographers and guidebook authors.

Vicky is the author of *Cross-Country Ski Tours of Washington's North Cascades, 100 Hikes in California's Central Sierra and Coast Range,* and *Bicycling the Pacific Coast.* Tom is author/photographer of *Mountain Bike Adventures in Washington's South Cascades and Olympics* and *Washington's North Cascades and Puget Sound,* all published by The Mountaineers.

THE MOUNTAINEERS, founded in 1906, is a nonprofit outdoor activity and conservation club, whose mission is "to explore, study, preserve, and enjoy the natural beauty of the outdoors. . . ." Based in Seattle, Washington, the club is now the third-largest such organization in the United States, with 15,000 members and four branches throughout Washington State.

The Mountaineers sponsors both classes and year-round outdoor activities in the Pacific Northwest, which include hiking, mountain climbing, ski-touring, snowshoeing, bicycling, camping, kayaking and canoeing, nature study, sailing, and adventure travel. The club's conservation division supports environmental causes through educational activities, sponsoring legislation, and presenting informational programs. All club activities are led by skilled, experienced volunteers, who are dedicated to promoting safe and responsible enjoyment and preservation of the outdoors.

The Mountaineers Books, an active, nonprofit publishing program of the club, produces guidebooks, instructional texts, historical works, natural history guides, and works on environmental conservation. All books produced by The Mountaineers are aimed at fulfilling the club's mission.

If you would like to participate in these organized outdoor activities or the club's programs, consider a membership in The Mountaineers. For information and an application, write or call The Mountaineers, Club Headquarters, 300 Third Avenue West, Seattle, Washington 98119; (206) 284-6310.

Send or call for our catalog of more than 300 outdoor titles:

The Mountaineers Books
1001 SW Klickitat Way, Suite 201
Seattle, WA 98134
1-800-553-4453